Pandeiro Basics

Brazilian Rhythms: Choro, Samba, Baião & More

by Ami Molinelli

WWW.MELBAY.COM

Preface

This book is a guide to understanding the complex and multi-faceted instrument known as the pandeiro. It is with great care and deliberation that this book was created as an instructional manual and as an introduction to the instrument and many Brazilian musical styles with cultural references and brief histories to understand contextual use of each rhythm. Listening suggestions are provided to give context and are one snapshot of a myriad number of styles, examples, and musical references. As with any kind of cultural music or notation passed down by oral tradition, there are many paths and experts. Regional variances, even neighborhood variances are all accurate and true and part of oral tradition. This book is a compilation of 20 years of experience and information gathering with experts and research. It is a beginning but not a final or absolute history.

Best,
Ami Molinelli

Acknowledgements

Engraving by Anne Sajdera. Photographer Andy Mogg for images used in the book. Cover design by Joe Chellman at ShooFly Media.

Table of Contents: Pandeiro Adaptations, Volume 1

Chapter 1. A Brief History of Choro

What is choro music?
Choro is a style of Brazilian popular music that originated in Brazil in the late 1800s.

The first official small choro group was "O Choro do Calado" named after Joaquim Antônio da Silva Calado. Close to the year, 1870 choro was used as a title for instrumental groups consisting of flute, cavaquinho, and guitar. These groups played European dance/salon music and started to create new variations of dance and music.

Choro as a genre pre-dates samba and is considered the first national musical style of Brazilian origin. Brazilian performers presented European dance styles for salons, parties and events and eventually incorporated classical musical styles with African-influenced music and rhythms creating a new stylistic genre. African dances like the lundu and batuque as well as European polca and the Spanish habanera rhythms provided many of the stylistic, rhythmic, and structural ingredients.

Where was choro played or heard? Choro was often performed in salons or private events of the upper social classes. Waltzes, schottisches, mazurkas, polcas, and other European styles of music were studied and performed in the salons of the elite classes. Choro also evolved in musical style through military-style marching bands such as the "Banda do Corpo de Bombeiros," (Fireman's Corps Marching Band) led by choro pioneer, Anacleto de Madeiros. Marching bands also performed in town squares and public parks.

Who first played choro music? Choro musicians were amateur musicians who played mostly at festivals and/or were public or civil servants, military personnel, firefighters, postal workers, etc. Composers such as Anacleto de Madeiros were important in the evolution and history of choro. He wrote choro-style compositions for marching bands and big bands that included elaborate horn sections and incorporated marching band percussion such as cymbals, bass drum, and snare drums.

What was the first national music of Brazil? Maxixe was the first purely Brazilian music but is now considered part of the repertoire and under the umbrella of choro. Maxixe is considered the first national music of Brazil because it is the first music performed and played that was neither European nor African, but purely Brazilian.

What is maxixe? Maxixe is now considered part of the choro repertoire but maxixe was originally recognized as the first distinctly Brazilian music as well as a dance style. Maxixe has influences from the African lundu and the European polca and was seen as an indecent dance form because of the close physical contact between dancers. Chiquinha Gonzaga and Ernesto Nazareth were important composers who popularized the style. They also were both piano players so their independence of left-hand playing rhythmic contexts was definitive. Ernesto Nazareth did not call his compositions "maxixe" and labeled them "tango brasileiro." Maxixe is also a dance form that became popular around the world including Europe and the U.S.A. Initially, maxixe was considered indecent because of the dancing style. Couples were partnered and the dance had bodies closely dancing together with bodies touching instead of dancing with lots of space in between. Other factors such as who was dancing it, who was performing the music, and what class level factored as well. Maxixe would become a "trend" and "viral" and was known throughout Europe, the Americas and as far as Russia.

Why were some maxixes called "tango brasileiro?" Tango Brasileiro was a more accepted term for maxixe, initially, by the upper classes. Ernesto Nazareth called his compositions "tango brasileiro" but many are similar or identical to a maxixe. Ernesto Nazareth was a high-profile composer and pianist in the mid-1800s who was instrumental in moving choro music forward in Brazilian culture and identity. He often performed for the upper social classes and in the salons of the elite. Race and class were extremely divided and factored heavily into how music was labeled.

What is the form of choro? Choro is in rondo form and has three sections based on the classical sonata form, ABACA. There are also other variations such as AABBACCA for example. Most choros have three sections of music though some only have two. This is generally the form but of course there are many variations. It is very important for the pandeiro player to know the song and the form.

How does improvisation work in choro? Improvisation occurs in choro, but it is defined by the form and rhythm more strongly than jazz which can be more free-flowing. Improvising in choro is more about the theme and variation of the melody and section being soloed over. The solo can be passed over an A section or B section in a jam or "roda" and by signaling in advance by playing a bit of the section or calling out the section to solo over. In both classical music and in jazz, musicians might refer to the three sections of a song-form as "A, B or C" sections. However, in choro, the three sections are often referred to by number, "1, 2, or 3" and can be signaled by hands holding up 1, 2 or 3 fingers, shouting the number out loud that the soloist wants to solo over or have the band play, and/or playing a melodic pick-up that references and signals the actual section itself. Eye contact is essential for playing choro for this reason. The "head of a tune" is the same term in Portuguese known as the "cabeça" and that would be the first section.

What is the role of the pandeiro in improvisation for choro music? Pandeiro players absolutely need to know the form of the song and breaks of individual tunes. There is often less of a big "drum solo" but sometimes a short fill after a break. Sometimes the instrumental players will signal for the pandeiro player to take a section such as the last C or 3rd section which means knowing the form is essential. Sometimes the musicians will tag a line and play it over and over to let the pandeiro player solo.

Chapter 2. Traditional Choro Instrumentation

What is a Cavaquinho? The cavaquinho was brought to Brazil by the Portuguese and is descended from the Portuguese cavaquinho which is slightly larger and looks more like a small guitar. Sugar cane workers from Portugal (especially the island of Madeira) immigrated to Hawaii and brought the instrument there, where it evolved into the ukulele and is tuned differently and played with nylon strings. In choro and samba, the cavaquinho is traditionally tuned D-G-B-D and uses steel strings.

What is a Bandolim? The bandolim is Portuguese for mandolin and was brought to Brazil by the Portuguese.

What is a Violão 7-Cordas? The 7-string guitar is believed to have been brought to Brazil by Russian immigrants who performed in the circus. It allows for an extra bass string and is traditionally tuned to C.

Flauta (Flute), Clarinet and Saxophone: The flute and clarinet are traditional instruments in choro. Pixinguinha (originally a flute player) introduced the saxophone to choro music and it is now a standard instrument.

What is a Pandeiro? The pandeiro is a hand drum with concave jingles. It's part of the frame drum family. There are various styles of pandeiro used for different rhythms or musical styles and traditions throughout Brazil. Some examples of pandeiros are those made of plastic or nylon head pandeiros which are used in samba or pagode. Capoeira, an Afro-Brazilian martial art and dance form has its own style of pandeiro for accompaniment to capoeira and capoeira songs as well. In addition, jingles can be made of brass, chrome, or aluminum. Pandeiros for choro have a tunable skin head that is used with varying tones and accents and are customarily 10 inches.

What is a Caixeta? A caixeta is a wood block or piece of wood. The caixeta later evolved into the instrument known as a tamborim.

What is a Tamborim? A tamborim is a small frame drum played with a stick or "baqueta" and keeps the "ride" or "levada" in choro and samba. (See Chapter 18)

Additional Auxiliary Percussion - Afoxé and Reco-Reco: Afoxé is a small Afro-Brazilian gourd drum that fits in your hand and is covered with beads. It's also a rhythm and style of music. Rolling the afoxé in your hand creates a sound and can be used to play the maxixe rhythm. A reco-reco is a scraper either made of wood such as bamboo or metal springs and used in choro or samba.

Chapter 3. A Choro Glossary

Choro: Choro in Portuguese means to "cry." There are varying stories about the origins of the word, and one is that "choro" was a slang word used in common vernacular to "repeat" or copy something one just said or heard. Another explanation is that it was a slang term used to describe a guitar player's improvisations or style of playing and meant that the music was so beautiful being played that the guitar was "crying." The first documented use of a group using the word choro was associated with João Calado's trio and some believe the name stuck and was more widely used after that.

Choro Music: Choro is considered the first national music of Brazil. Choro is known for taking classical form and counterpoint melody from European salon music infused and mixed with African rhythms. Choro music was born in Rio de Janeiro. The first choro music and conjuntos did not include the pandeiro or percussion.

Regional: A group of choro musicians that make up an ensemble.

Conjuntos: Conjuntos were small groups of musicians playing choro music. Instrumentation in the first choro groups consisted of guitar or two guitars, cavaquinho, and flute.

Choro Gafiera: A choro gafiera band traditionally features an almost "big-band" type set up with a horn section and/or wind instruments like the clarinet or flute, rhythm section of percussion (pandeiro, tan tam, drum set, etc.) bass, keyboards, guitar, and cavaquinho. Gafiera can range in size from as little as six people to a fuller big band of 15 or 20 or more musicians. Choro gafiera is a ballroom-style dance that evolved from the maxixe dance and includes several rhythm styles such as polca, maxixe, lundu, choro and samba as well as others.

Roda: Roda in Portuguese means a circle and signifies a "jam" session. Players usually sit in a circle or around a table. Who calls the song might signify who leads the form of the song.

Rondo Form: Rondo form is used often in certain styles of traditional classical music and signifies that there are three sections of a composition and that the form is AABBACCA or another similar variation. This is the typical form most choros use yet they can vary slightly. In a choro jam or "roda" musicians may improvise over the melody of a section and will signal which section they want to play by giving a verbal or hand gesture signal of "1, 2, and 3" and hold up 1, 2 or 3 fingers instead of "A, B and/or C." Another way to cue is to hint at the section through your instrument as a pick-up at the end of another section.

Side Note: *One note of interest is that the famous composition, "Carinhoso" by Pixinguinha is only two sections. He wrote the composition in 1917 and left it aside because it had only two sections. The story has it that he left it in a drawer for more than 20 years until he gave it to João de Barro in 1937. It was used in a very popular telenovela (soap opera) in the 1970s and became a hit once again.*

Classical Music Terms Used in Choro

Dynamics: Dynamics in music describe the volume of music. Choro is traditionally acoustic so making sure to understand the dynamics of the music is important. Using soft and loud dynamics is essential to choro music and knowing which **phrase** to play more strongly or more softly is important to the music and expression.

Piano: Piano is an Italian word for soft used in classical music and tells the performer to play quietly. "p" is written on sheet music (score) under the phrasing that is directed to be played softly. Pianissimo is "very soft" and is signaled with "pp."

Forte: Forte is an Italian word for loud. The symbol is "f." Fortissimo is very loud and the symbol is "ff."

Mezzo-Forte: Mezzo means "medium" and mezzo-forte means moderately loud. The symbol is mf.

Mezzo-Piano: Mezzo means "medium" and mezzo-piano means moderately soft. The symbol is mp.

Ritardando: A gradual decrease of speed often at the end of a song for emotional impact or at the start.

Rallentando: A gradual decrease of speed often at the end of a song for emotional impact or at the start.

Rubato: This means out of time and sometimes the start or end of a tune for a short time. It allows for an expression of slackening the time and in choro will be spelled out in the chart, in the arrangement or on cue.

Accelerando: Speeding up often on cue.

Crescendo: To gradually increase in volume from piano to forte.

Decrescendo: To gradually decrease in volume from forte to piano. It looks like the "less than" sign.

Diminuendo: This is similar to a decrescendo. Officially it means to "diminish" the sound gradually.

Tag: In choro to "tag an ending" means to cue or play the last phrase repeatedly. At the end of a song, the cue the ending, musicians might play the last phrase three times and that means they are "tagging" it.

Fill: A break or pause at the end of a phrase for example, for a musician to improvise a short idea. For example, in choro there might be space at the end of one section of music for the pandeiro player or musician to fill one to two measures of music before the next section starts with an improvised fill. This is often done on cue and sometimes is written into an arrangement.

Chapter 4. A Brief Pandeiro History in Choro

When did the pandeiro become introduced to choro?
The pandeiro was first introduced to choro in the early 1900s. Pixinguinha's group, "Os Oito Batutas" was first photographed with a pandeiro in 1919 with Jaco Palmeira. The band consisted of Pixinguinha on flute, Donga on guitar, Jose Alves on mandolin and shaker, China on guitar and piano, Nelson Alves on cavaco, Luis de Oliveira on bandola and reco-reco, and Raul Palmieri on guitar to name a few of the musicians. They were also the first group to go abroad to France in 1921.

What are the origins of the pandeiro?
In the Northeast of Brazil in San Luis, there is a tradition and musical style called "bumba-meu-boi." The drum used in this style is a large and square-looking frame drum, called an adufe, also known as a "pandeiro quadrado" (square pandeiro). The adufe is similar to a square frame drum found in Egypt that dates back to 1400 B.C. These drums were first brought to Brazil by the Portuguese and played by Portuguese Catholic women. They can range in size from 12 to 24 inches with a typical adufe around 17.5 inches.

What are the origins of frame drums?
The word "adufe" comes from the Arabic word "duff" or "deff," a term used in the Middle Ages to describe a round or square frame drum. It's important to note that the tambourine, a percussion instrument, is found in many Mediterranean, African and Middle-Eastern cultures.

Much of the history of the tambourine is traced to the Moorish culture using this instrument throughout their empire and traveling with it to Portugal. The history of the adufe goes back to the time of the Moors when they were brought to Portugal in the early 700s A.D. during the invasion of the Iberian Peninsula. In addition, Mediterranean texts refer to religious frame drums being played by women from Egypt, through Greece, and Rome.

Are there pandeiros in other cultures and how did the name evolve?
It is believed that the actual word "pandeiro" evolved from the Persian-Arabic name for a frame drum called a bendayer (ben-dair).

In Spain and Galicia there are square frame drums called "pandeiros." Other terms used are the "pandeireta" or "pandir." In Puerto Rico there is a "pandereta" and in Mexico there is "pandero jarocho." In the United States, the gospel tambourines used in African-American churches and Mardi Gras are made with natural drumheads, however the jingles are convex and not concave and usually chrome.

Chapter 5. Choosing a Pandeiro and Amplification

Choro pandeiro: Choro is played with a pandeiro that has an animal skin head and a wooden frame. The jingles are usually made of brass but can also be chrome. The wooden frame pandeiro is used for styles like choro, acoustic music, and acoustic samba/roots samba or "samba de raiz." Instrumentation is often played with acoustic instruments such as the guitar, mandolin, clarinet, cavaquinho or known as a cavaco and flute. In traditional choro, the pandeiro is the only percussion instrument in the ensemble.

Some luthiers who make pandeiros have their own personal and individual style. Depending on the thickness of the head of the drum, a pandeiro player can create different tones out of the animal skin head. Some luthiers are known for their specific skill of making jingles, wooden frames, and the lightness of the drum.

Capoeira pandeiro: The capoeira pandeiros are also wood pandeiros with an animal skin head but are used specifically for use in the martial art/dance of capoeira with rhythms such as afoxé. The pandeiros are used to accompany the capoeiristas traditional movements in a "roda" and accompany the Brazilian berimbau (a musical bow instrument) with songs. Traditionally these instruments are also handmade but sometimes simpler in design with recycled bottle caps for jingles and lesser quality skins for the head of the drum.

Samba pandeiro: These instruments are made with a plastic head and have wooden or synthetic frames. They are most often used in samba or pagode and tuned to a higher pitch than the choro pandeiro. They are designed to be louder to be played in pagode, a style of music with a large percussion section or with amplified instruments and to compete with a larger percussion section and even drum set.

How to choose a pandeiro: Many players use different pandeiros for different styles of music. If playing pagode or samba, then most likely, a pandeiro with a plastic head is recommended.

Using a Microphone

Using a microphone: The pandeiro can be amplified with a clip-on microphone. There are a few different models that are available on the market. Many pandeiro players use an Audio Technica 35 model which is what I prefer and it comes with a gooseneck clip-on mic and needs phantom power. Almost any amplifier will have a phantom power button but if not, they sell an additional phantom box you can plug into in case the board or amp does not. Shure SM98 is another common clip-on microphone pandeiro players use. German based company, Valter percussion makes a pandeiro mic that looks a lot like the Audio Technica and is also a gooseneck with phantom power and is designed for the pandeiro.

Microphones for pandeiros aren't often used in a roda or small jam. If so, then just for the 7-string guitar player to be heard above a range of other instruments. If on stage or in a performance where amplification is necessary, it's important to strive for a balanced sound of the base notes and jingles.

On-stage microphone: If using a plastic head pandeiro having an overhead microphone can suffice but for the choro pandeiro (natural skin head) just putting a mic from above the pandeiro will capture mostly jingles and high tones. Amplifying the pandeiro from underneath ensures the deepest base sound vs. just hearing the jingles.

Recording: Getting the right sample is important, always bring in an example track to help an engineer who might be unfamiliar with the sound of the instrument or what it's supposed to sound like. In a recording studio, always record with two microphones to capture the top and bottom sounds.

Chapter 6. How to Properly Hold the Pandeiro

Most people who are right-handed hold the pandeiro with their left hand. The drum should feel secure in your hand.

Holding the drum with the left hand

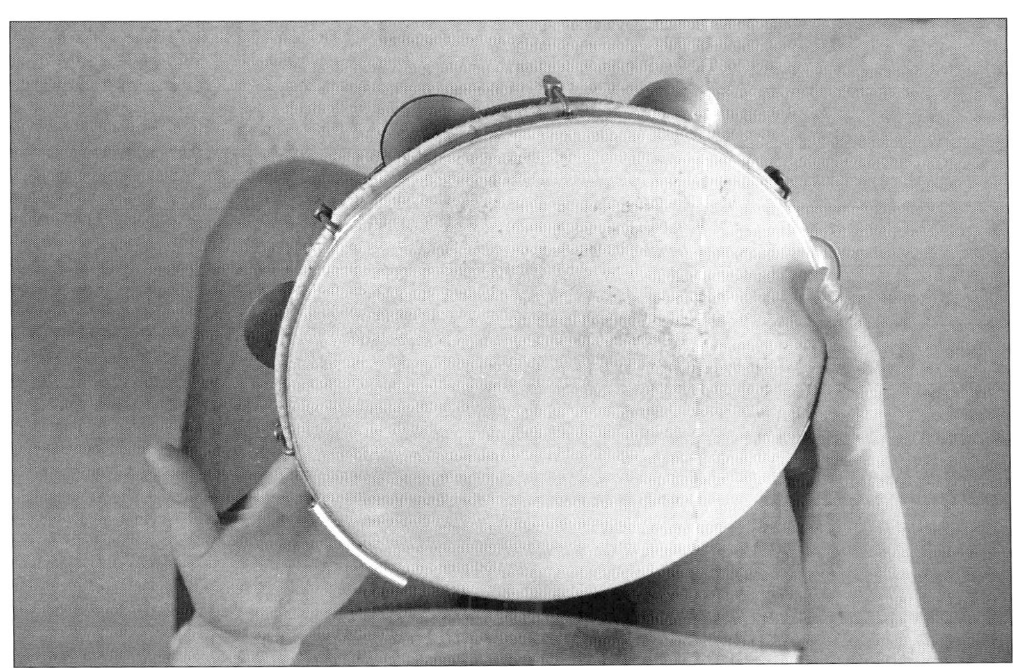

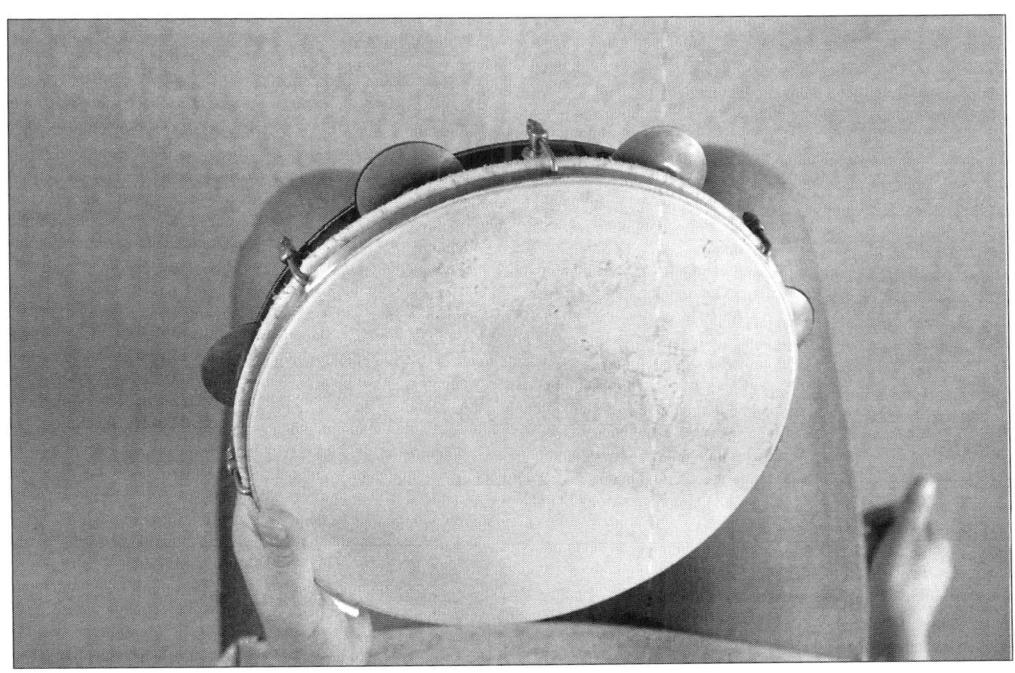

Another view of the left hand

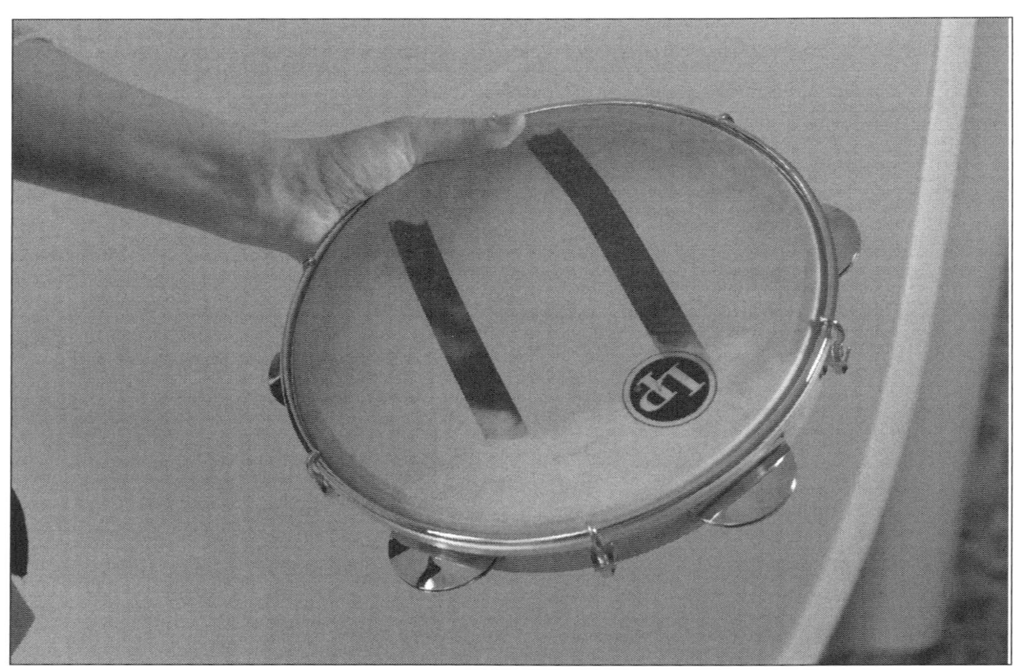

Bottom of the pandeiro

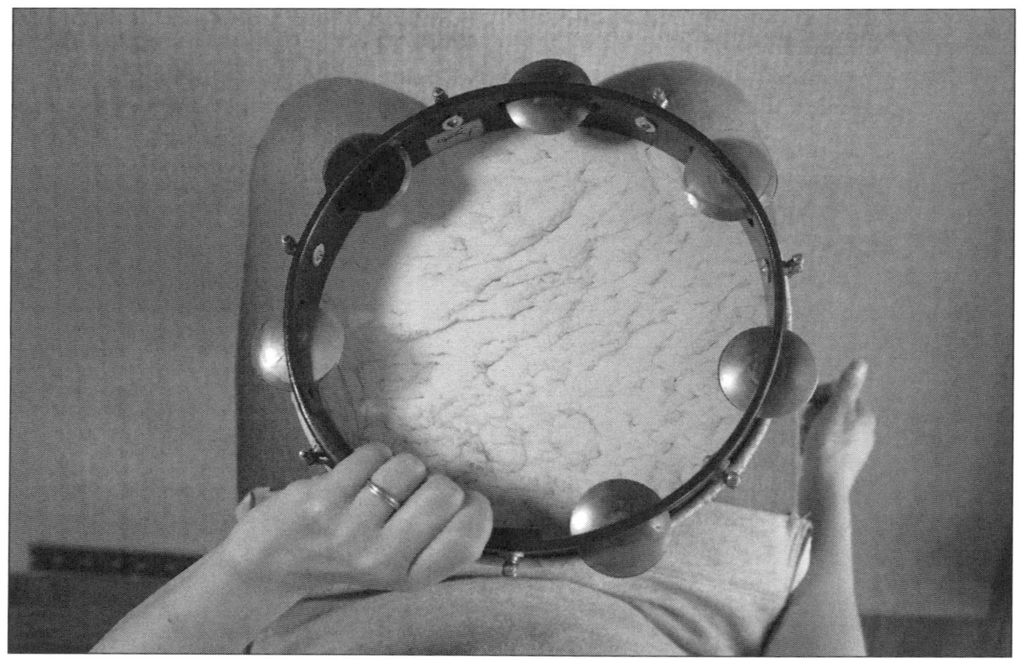

Top of the pandeiro where the right hand should be placed

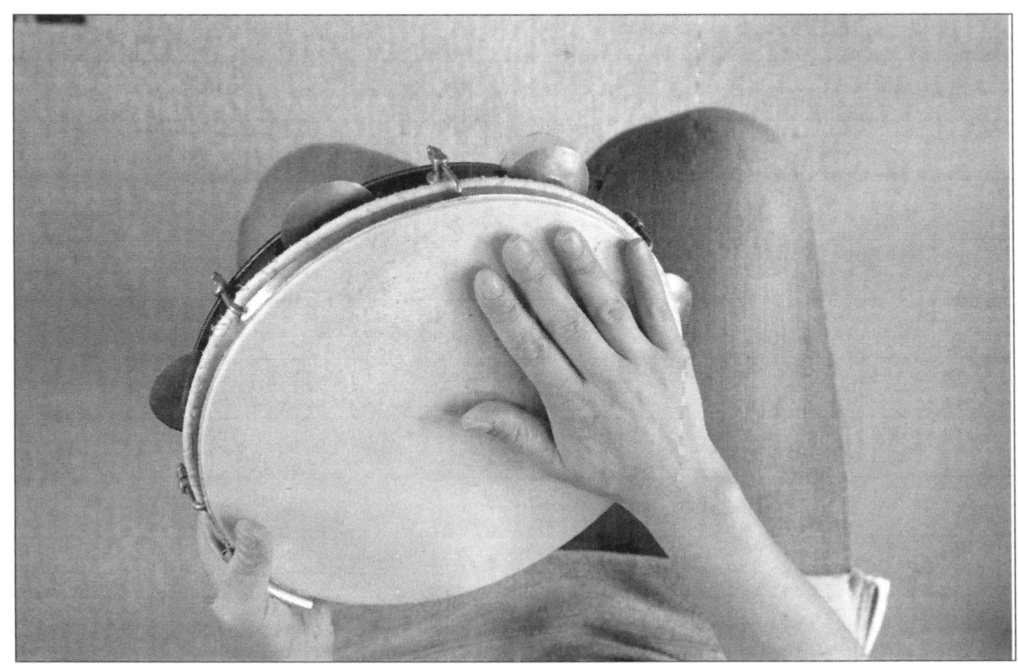

Another view of where the right hand should be placed

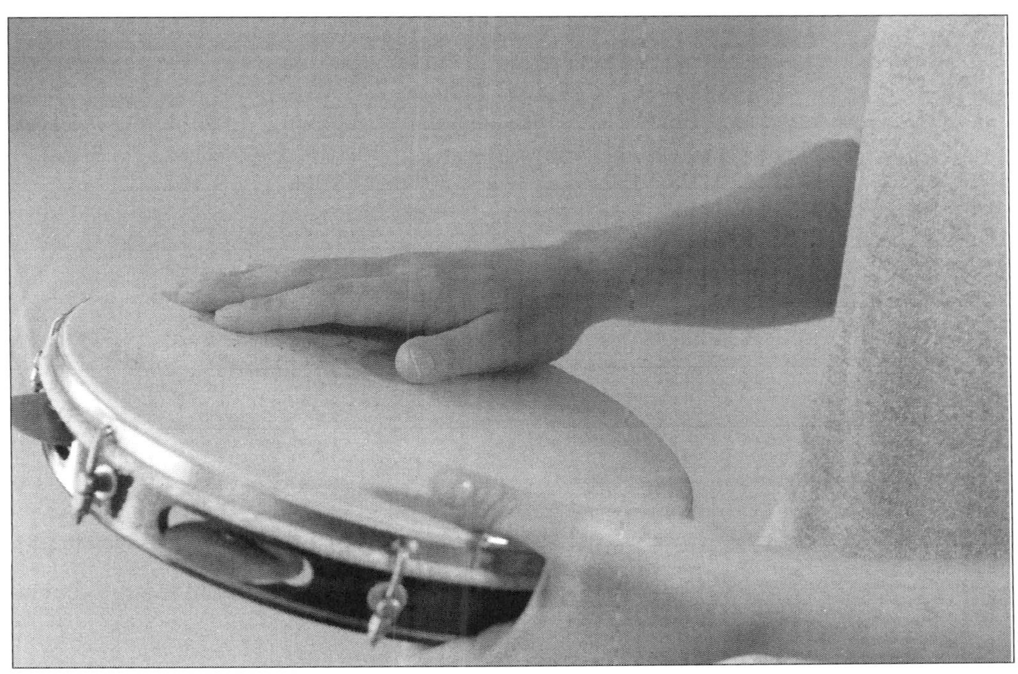

Hitting the pandeiro for a bass tone with the thumb

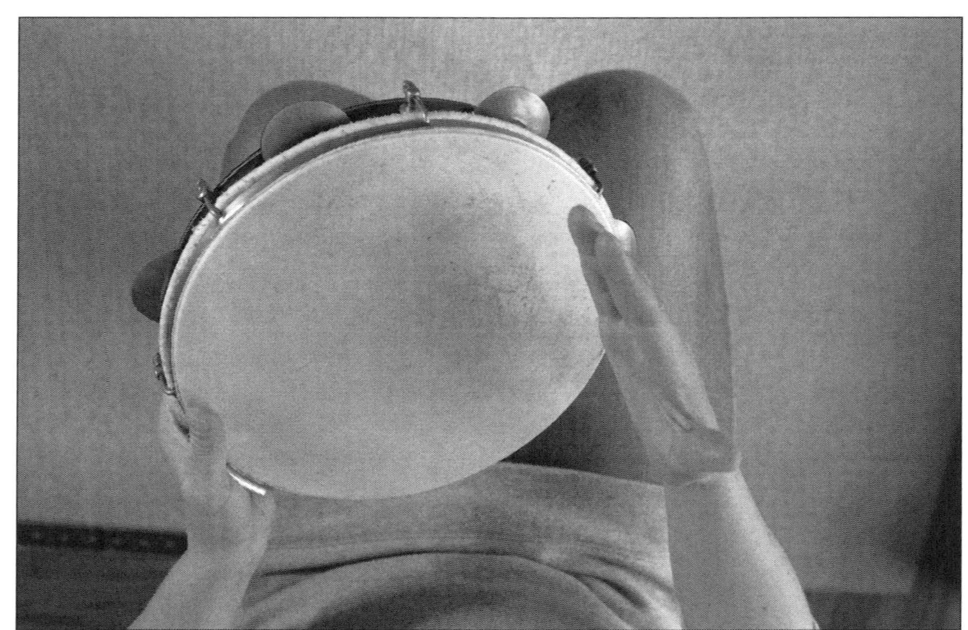

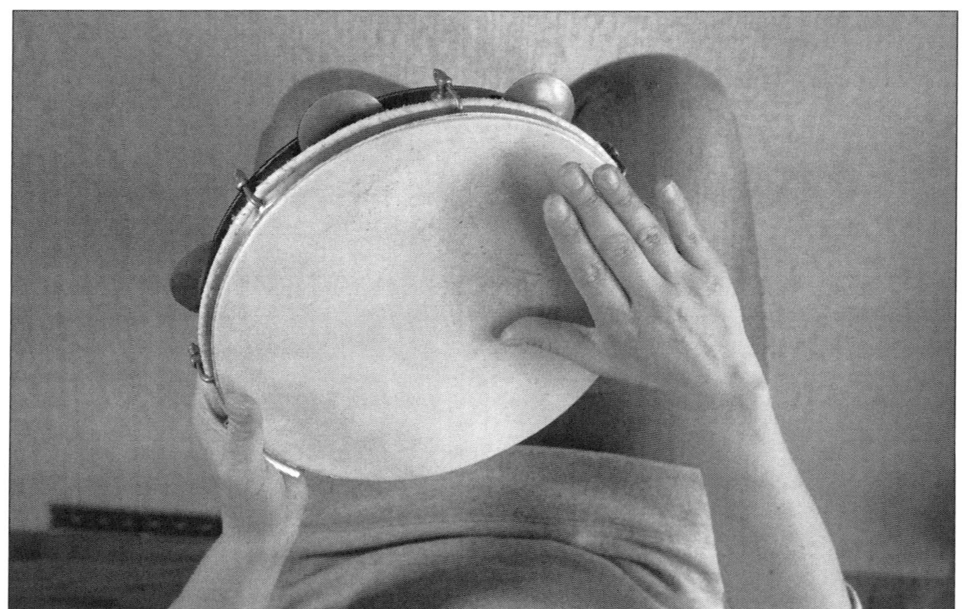

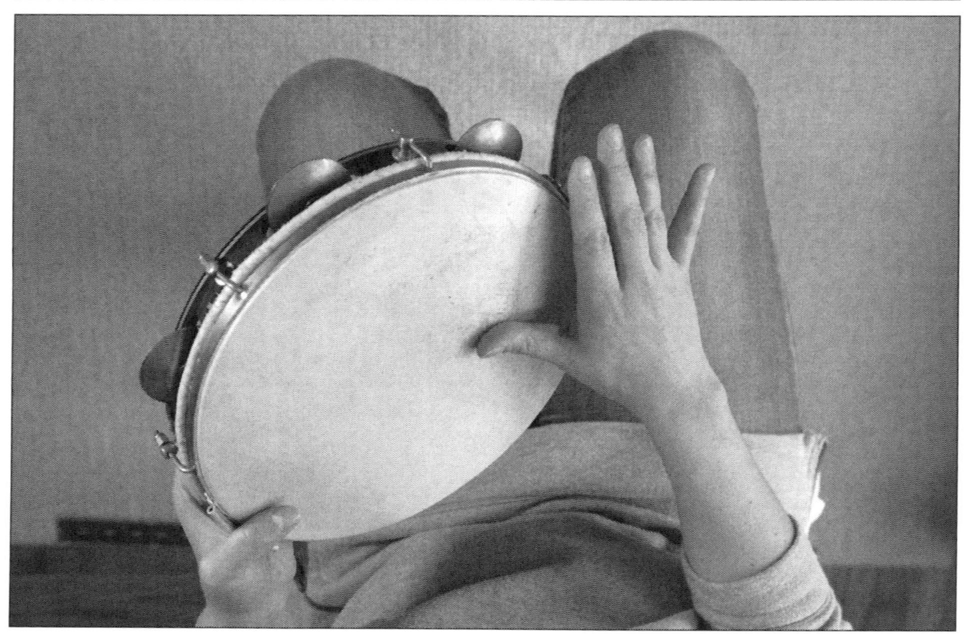

Hitting the pandeiro with the fingertips

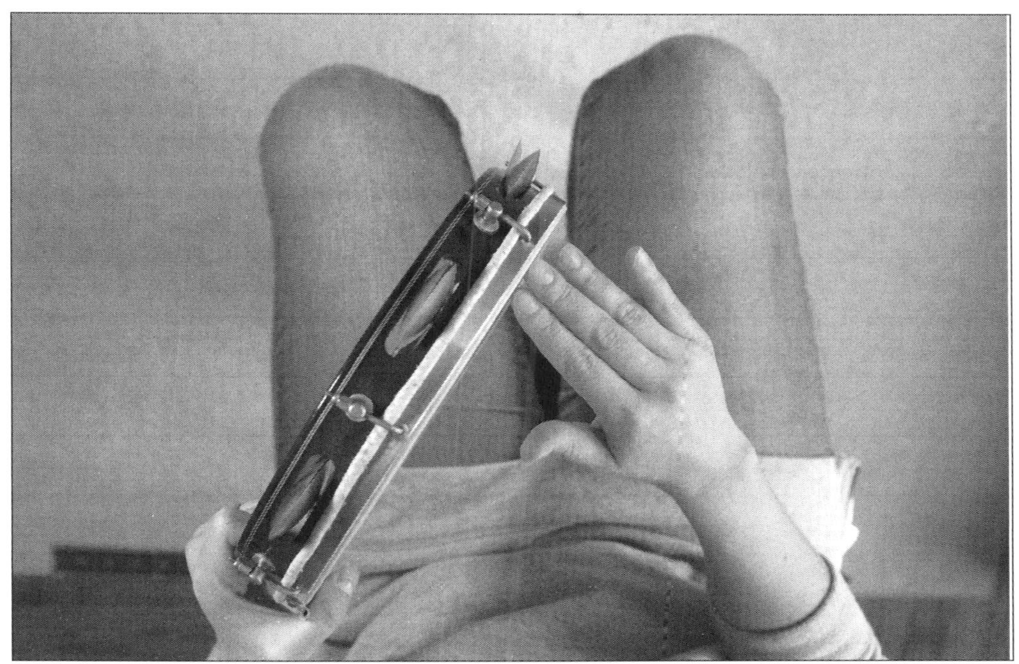

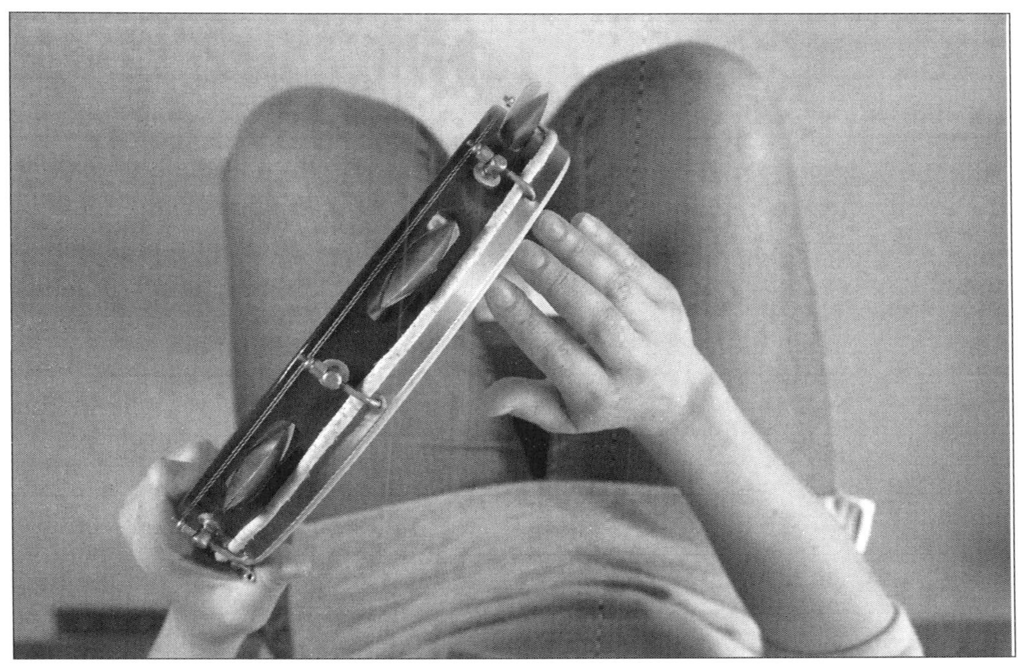

Hitting the pandeiro with the heel of the hand

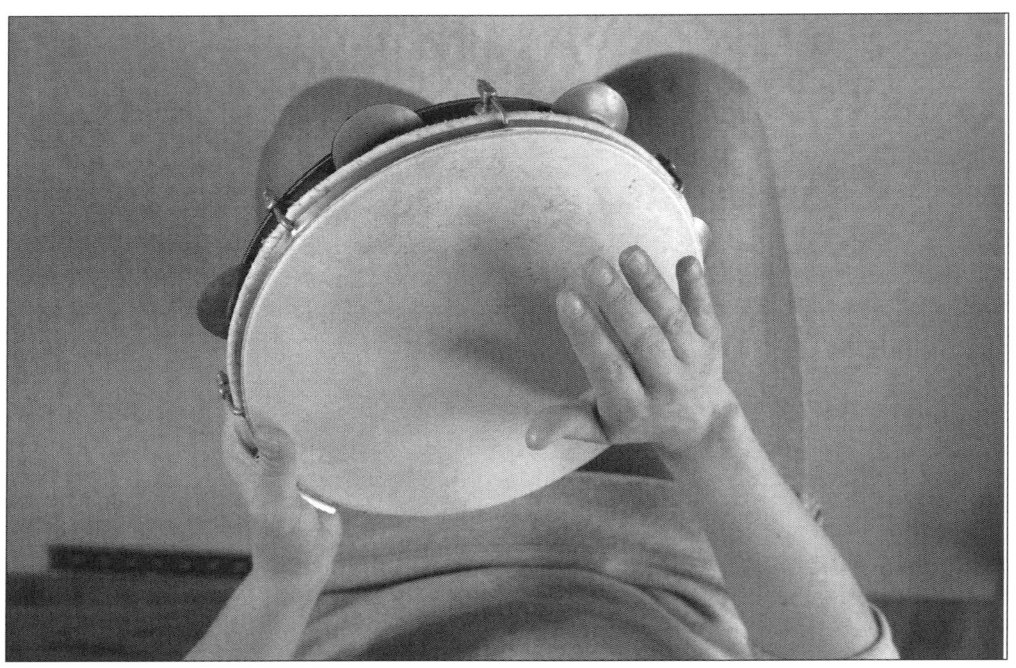

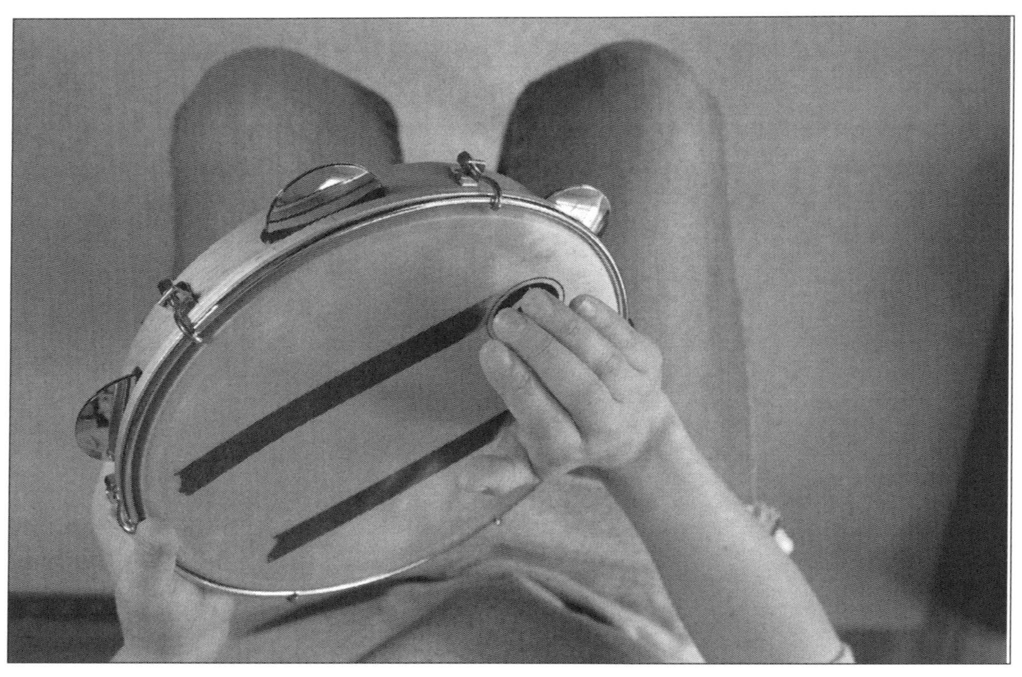

Open and Closed Notes:

Traditionally the closed note in choro is felt on beat 1 and the open accent on beat 2 of the most basic choro rhythm. The thumb or tip can be played as an open note or muted. To mute the note, press the third or middle finger to the bottom of the pandeiro with your less dominant hand that holds the pandeiro. For right-handed players that means holding the pandeiro with your left hand and vice versa for left-handed players. Open notes require you to lift the finger to unmute the drum. Maintain a good grip so that you have the flexibility to open and close using that finger. Some players may use their ring finger but it's most common to use the middle finger.

Bottom of the pandeiro with mute

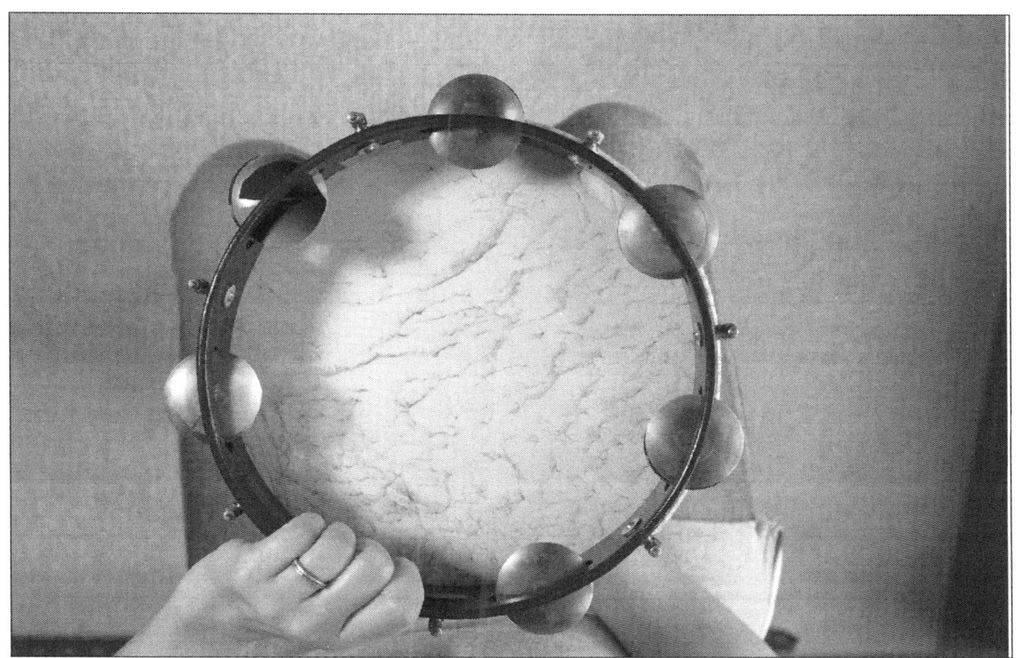

Bottom of the pandeiro without mute

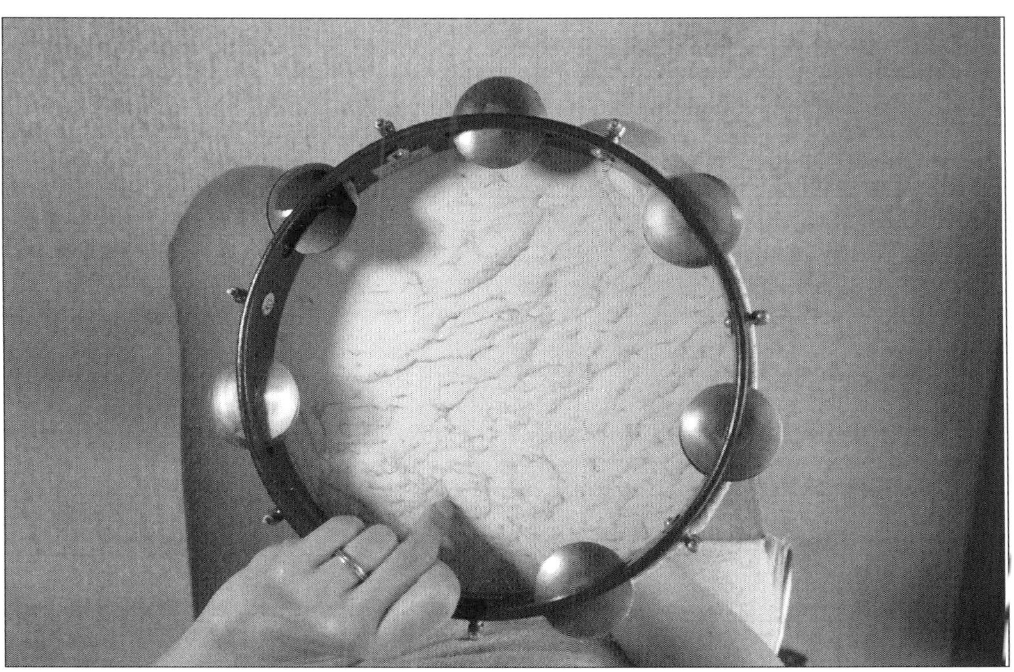

Hitting a Slap: Whole Hand vs. Thumb

Traditionally hitting a slap on the choro pandeiro is used more frequently in pagode or samba. There are two ways to execute a slap on the pandeiro. The first with the whole hand takes the place of where your tips would normally slap and can be best explained as if you were clapping your hands but just holding the pandeiro in the left hand.

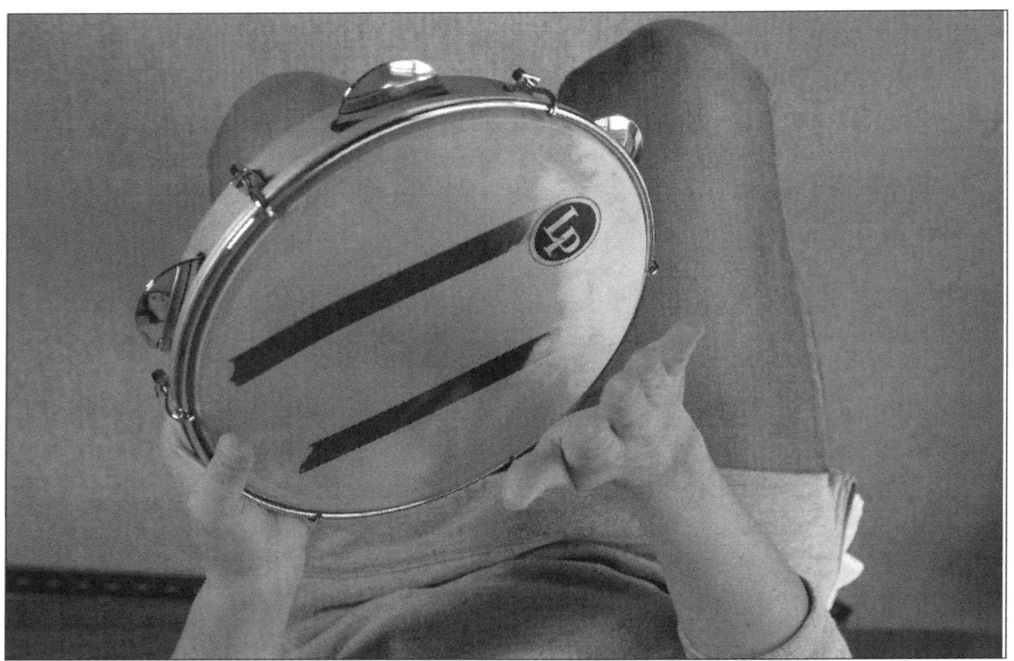

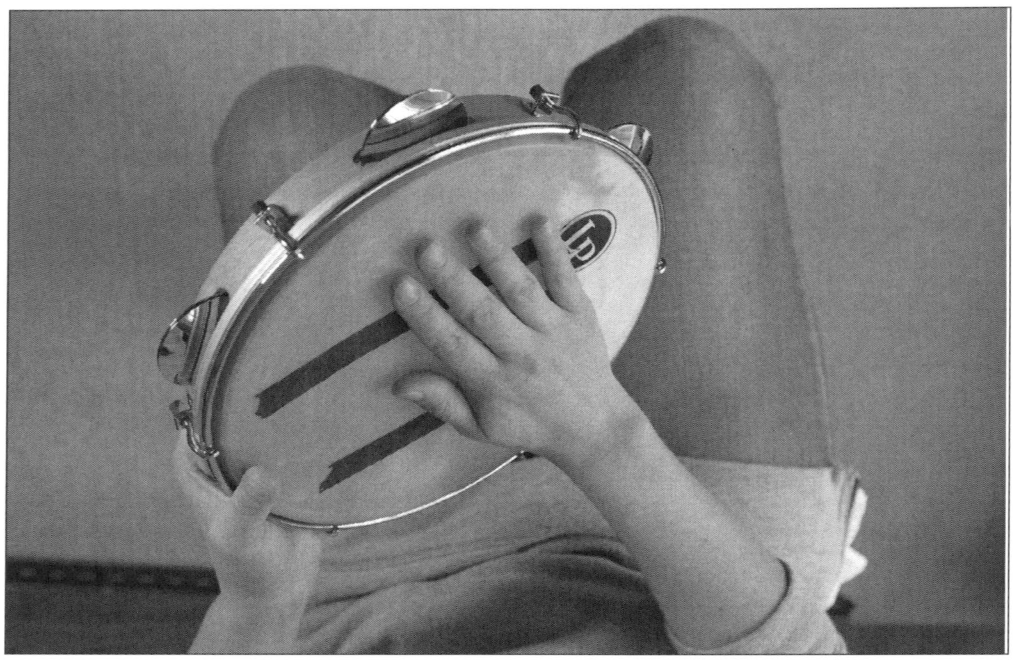

Hitting a slap with your thumb is going to be different because you are only using your thumb and not the whole hand. When you play the Northeastern or Funk examples that begin with starting the pattern on your fingertips or tips, this will be the best way to execute a constant 16th-note motion and learn to hit a thumb-slap. It requires hinging downward and hitting the center of the drum.

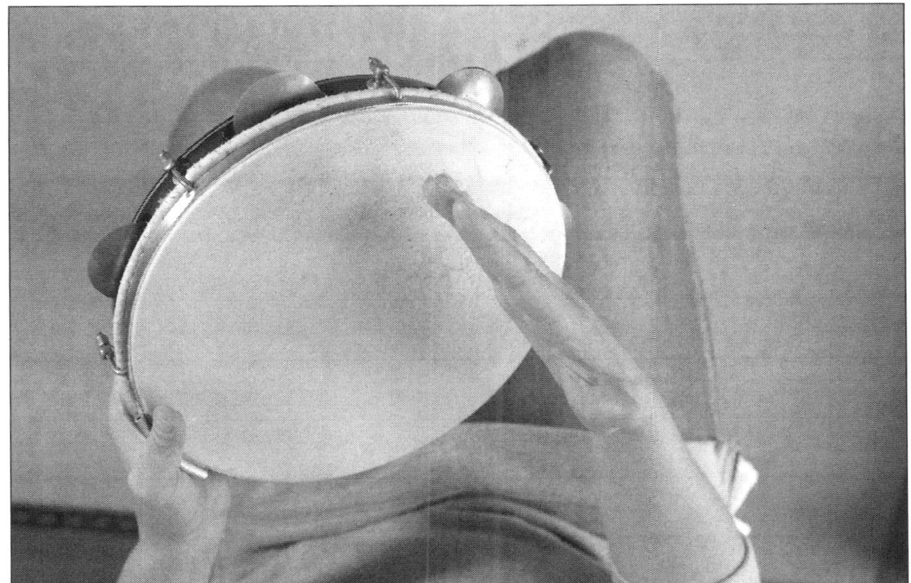

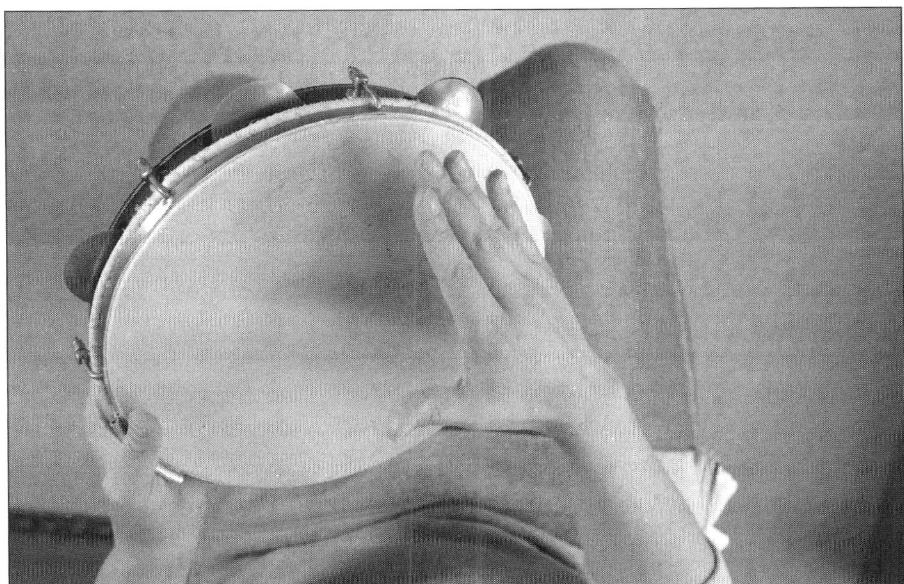

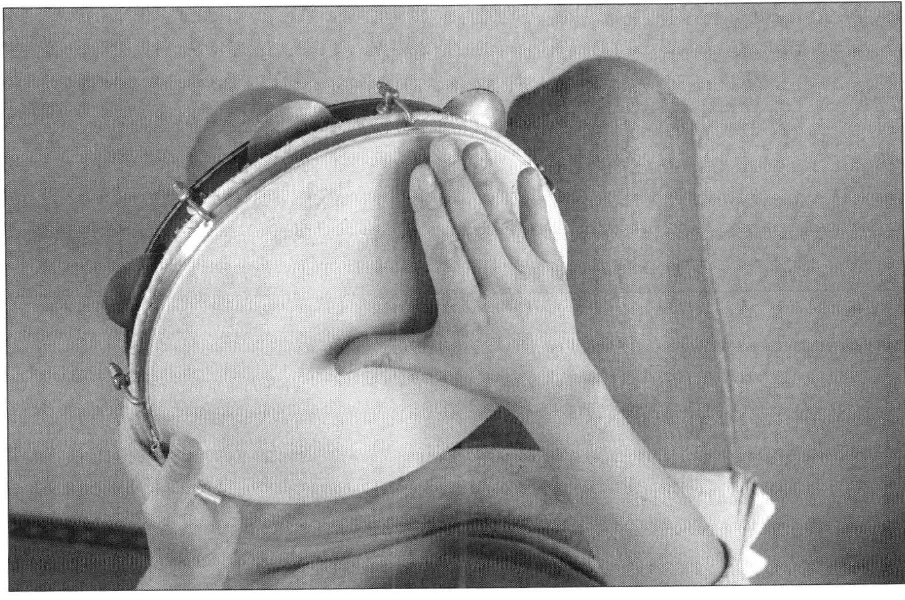

Chapter 7. Technique and Guide

Notation Key

Thumb	**TH**
Tip	**t**
Heel	**h**
Slap	**SL**
Trill	**Tr**

Closed note (tips, thumb, or heel)

Th or t or h

Open note (tips or thumb)

Th or t

Half-open (tip or thumb)

Th or t

Slap (tip slap or thumb slap)

SL or Th (SL)

Trill (also known as a roll)

Tr = with tips

Accent >

(Accent on any note but usually never on heel)

Chapter 8. More About Pandeiros & Avoiding Injury

Sitting: If sitting, percussionists playing any instrument should be seated on a stool or the edge of a seat with both feet flat on the ground. Hitting a drum is repetitive motion and being as symmetrical as possible will help avoid any injury. The pandeiro should be in front of you about mid torso and equidistant between both hands (middle of your body).

Standing: When standing, keep your feet hip-width apart and stand straight without leaning against anything. Arms should be relaxed and the drum mid-torso.

Pain: If at any point you feel pain, then something is wrong. Pain from hitting the rim, jingles or drum is not something to get used to, it's something to adjust. In addition, if your wrist starts to hurt and it will be sore at the beginning of the left-hand rotation then practice a little, stretch your arms, and work up to more speed and longevity.

Carpal Tunnel Syndrome: If you practice your left-hand technique then you will avoid a lot of carpal tunnel injuries. If you already have issues with this or an injury, consult your doctor and proceed cautiously or wait until you are healed.

Pandeiro Rims: Depending on your pandeiro, some have a round rim and some a flat rim. Regardless of the rim you should not be hitting the metal edge or rim with your fingers or hand. This will cause injury and pain and just hit the skin on the instrument.

Use a Mirror: This is the best way to check posture and placement. A mirror is very useful to make sure the pandeiro is not raised too high or too low but held in the center of the torso or a little lower.

How to Practice: There are many ways to practice and one of them is with a metronome. The metronome is important but also find music you enjoy that is the right tempo for where you can sustain playing for an entire song. When I first learned to play pandeiro, my first goal was to play a samba pattern for a whole song at a medium tempo. I couldn't finish a song for several weeks without stopping and I had to work up to it. I still practice regularly to maintain my agility with a fast tempo. If I don't play for a week, I lose some of my agility. I always suggest playing for a shorter period daily (even 15-20 minutes) in comparison to practicing only one hour once a week.

Pandeiro Size: This is probably the biggest source of confusion for new pandeiro players. As mentioned previously, pandeiros are different sizes and weights. A typical choro pandeiro is 10 inches. There are multiple sizes for pandeiro including, 8-inch pandeiros up to 11, 12 and 14 inches. Customarily though 14 inch is very large and not traditional for choro but is used more for pagode or samba. 8-inch pandeiros are great for kids to learn on but not adult hands. To learn the proper technique, and to adjust to the most common choro pandeiro, the 10-inch pandeiro is standard. While there are 10-inch choro and samba pandeiros, 11 and 12-inch pandeiros are often used for samba or pagode.

Pandeiro Weight: Pandeiros also vary in weight depending on what material and hardware is used. Choro pandeiros made by a luthier tend to have more hand-made hardware and are kept as light as possible. When first learning to play, any pandeiro is possible but having a lighter pandeiro will help with the process.

Chapter 9. Warm-Ups with 16th Note Rotation for Choro & Samba

Without the left-hand rotation, your right hand will fatigue. It's important to engage both hands in playing by learning to rotate the left hand. While challenging at first, your technique, form and stamina will improve with time. Without spending some time learning the technique of the left-hand rotation it will be more difficult later to acquire it. This is a good exercise to practice using your left hand. Jorginho do Pandeiro, a great legendary pandeiro player who performed with Jacob do Bandolim and his band as well as his legacy group, Época de Ouro, developed and played with this style and is a defining example of choro pandeiro playing

Example 1: 16th Note Rotation

Example 2: 16th Note Rotation Adding Thumb

Chapter 10. Warm-Up Exercises for Tone Development

These exercises will help train both your tips and thumbs to have equal ability to hit a muted, open or slap tone. Groupings of 3 are also great for beginning improvisation.

Warm-Up Exercise 1: (Muted and closed starting on the thumb)

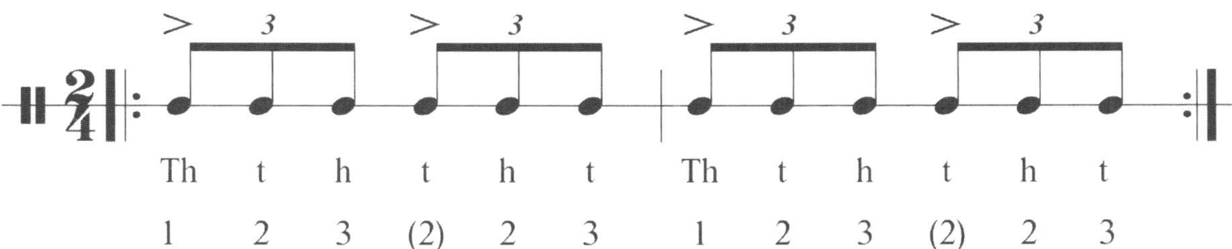

Warm-Up Exercise 2: (Muted and closed starting on the tip)

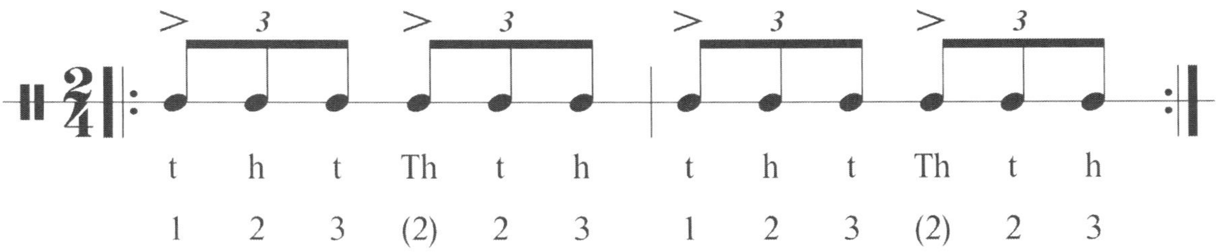

Warm-Up Exercise 3: (Open tone with open thumb)

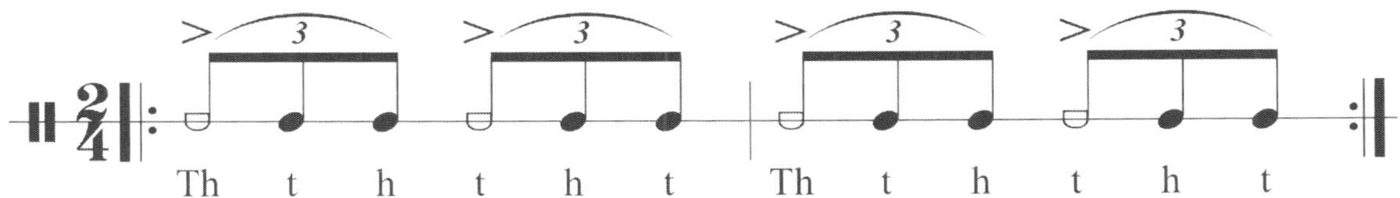

Warm-Up Exercise 4: (Open tone with open tip)

Try to make the middle and ring finger the focus as you hit the drum for an open note. Try to make the open tips sound like the open thumb.

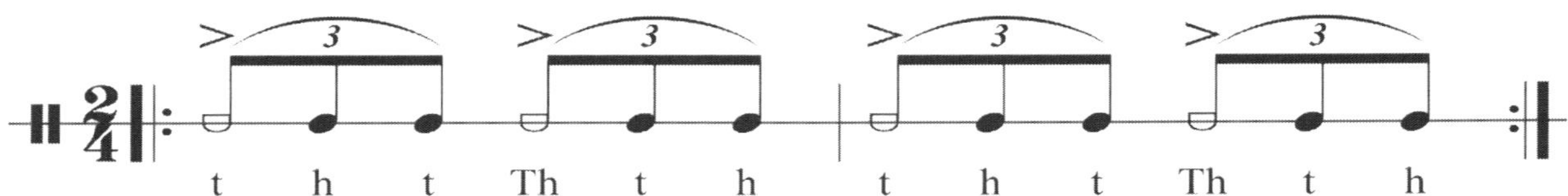

Warm-Up Exercise 5: (Playing with a slap)

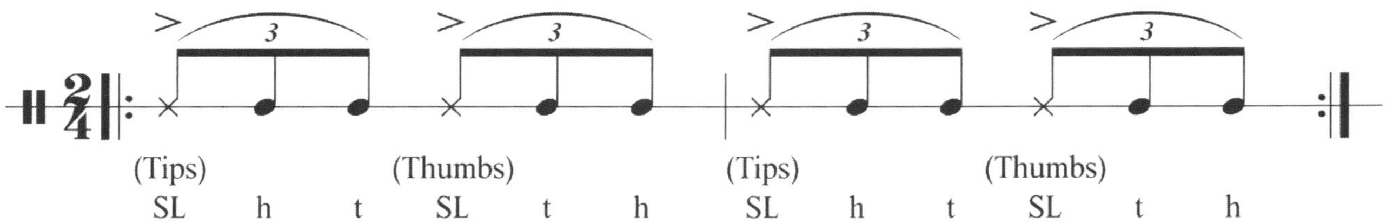

Warm-Up Exercise 6: (Playing with a slap, start on thumb)

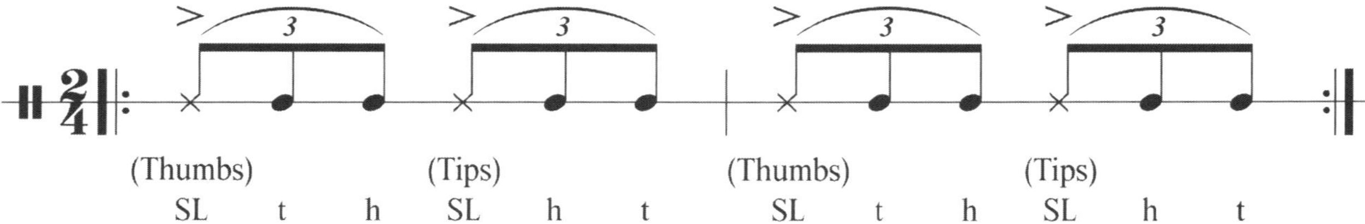

Chapter 11. Choro and Samba Fingering with 16th Note Rotation

Brazilian music is typically written in 2/4 instead of 4/4, except for bossa nova. In this book, pandeiro notation will be written in mostly 2/4 as well.

This is the basic choro or samba rhythm without accents but with correct fingering and using 16th note rotation.

16th Note Rotation with basic choro pattern

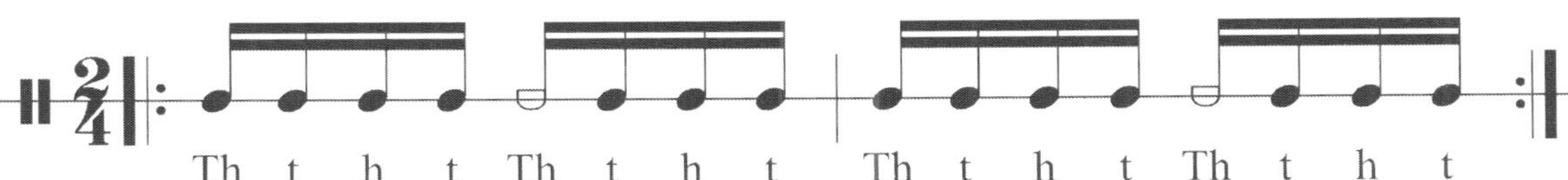

Reminder for practice

Keep each 16th note of the pandeiro equal in accent while playing the groove so that every note or pulse is felt equally. It's important that each 16th note has an equal value. Once you can play each note equally, then it's easier to execute the accents

Chapter 12. Accents for the Choro and Samba Patterns

The pandeiro accents a bass note on beat 2 like a surdo drum. The surdo or bass drum in choro or samba is always accented on beat 2. Beat "one" is closed and beat "two" is open. Both choro and samba music have this in common.

Sometimes the pandeiro can emphasize the "e" of the following pattern, while still keeping the groove, accents, and constant 16th note rotation. Bossa nova highly references accenting the "a" like the second example. Older choro and samba recordings, especially, choro will accent the "e" of beats 1 and 2 while still keeping a samba groove. Bossa nova highly references accenting the "a" of beats 1 and 2 as seen in the second example.

Example 1: Choro accents on "e"

Th t h t Th t h t Th t h t Th t h t
1 e & a 2 e & a 1 e & a 2 e & a

Example 2: Choro accents on "e" and open note on beat 2

Th t h t Th t h t Th t h t Th t h t
1 e & a 2 e & a 1 e & a 2 e & a

Example 3: Choro accents on "a" of beat 2 with an open tip

Th t h t Th t h t Th t h t Th t h t
1 e & a 2 e & a 1 e & a 2 e & a

Example 4: Basic choro rhythm: Putting together exercises 1-3

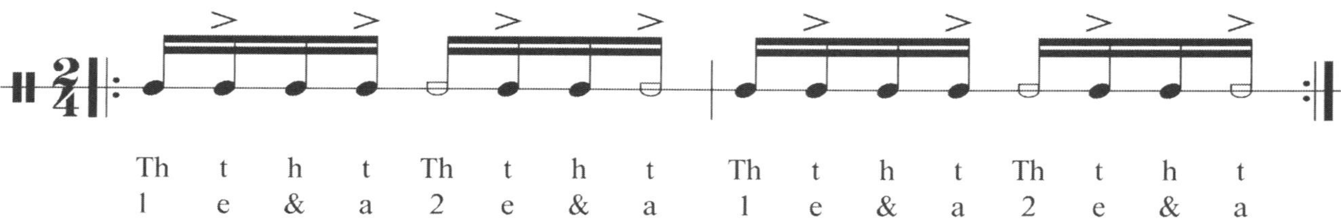

Th t h t Th t h t Th t h t Th t h t
1 e & a 2 e & a 1 e & a 2 e & a

Chapter 13. From Choro to Samba

Choro/Samba rhythm

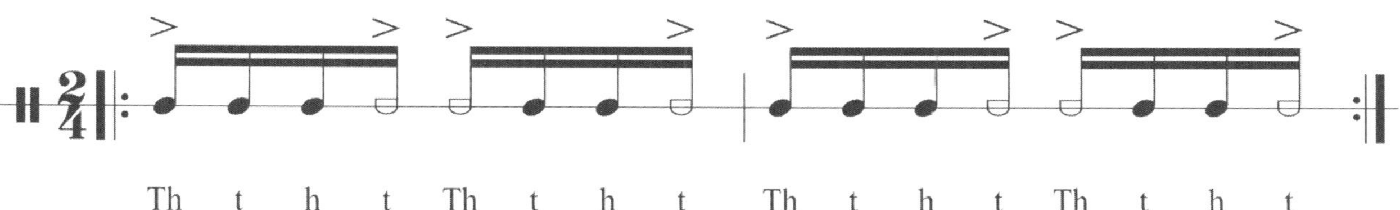

Adding a slap in the samba rhythm

Slaps aren't traditionally used in choro unless you are playing a "choro-samba," like "Noites Cariocas" by Jacob do Bandolim. As samba evolved, players changed the following pattern slightly. Slaps on a pandeiro are common for samba, pagode, partido alto, etc.

Samba pattern with added slap

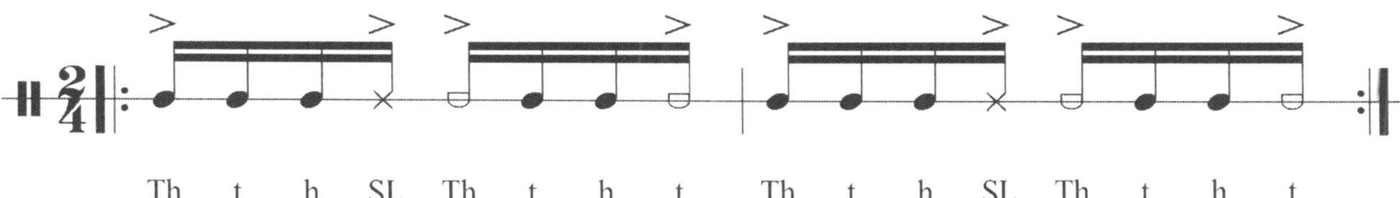

Chapter 14. Differing Hand/Finger Techniques for Playing Choro & Samba

Originally, the pandeiro was not played with the constant 16th note rotation in the left hand that one would typically see today for choro and samba, as discussed in Chapter 11. In addition, for pagode or partido alto, for example, the 16th note rotation doesn't apply to syncopated rhythms and technique. Many samba players use a different technique of "double thumbs" to play the basic samba pattern as well.

Double Thumbs

Carlinhos Pandeiro de Ouro, a virtuosic sambista and percussionist, gained early fame as the child pandeiro player featured in the original movie "Orfeu Negro" (Black Orpheus). Carlinhos Pandeiro de Ouro is revered as a master dancer and pandeiro player, or rather "sambista" and "pandeirista." He plays samba with the following pattern.

Marcos Suzano Technique

Marcos Suzano revitalized the instrument in the 1980s and re-popularized the use of the 16th note rotation. He plays the pattern starting on his tips instead and here is one example of a basic samba pattern starting on the tips.

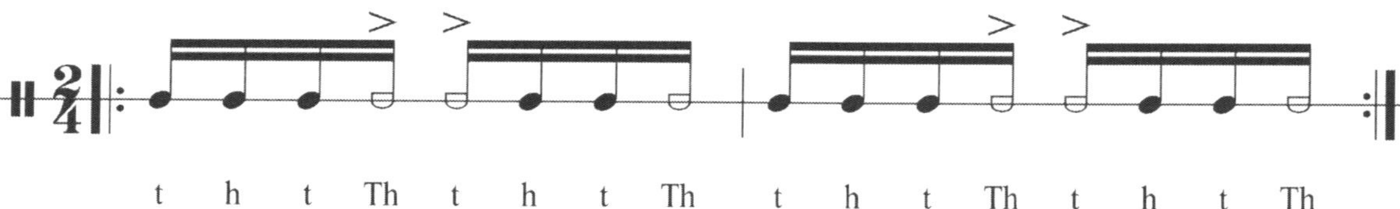

Chapter 15. Beginning Improvisation

When playing choro or samba, it helps to think of the surdo (bass drum), which is what the bass (open) notes on the pandeiro are accenting. Practice listening to surdo patterns and then try to adapt them for the pandeiro. The basic samba pattern accents the role of the surdo with the thumb but to create fills that mimic the surdo, the pandeiro player will either need to use the thumb in repetition or start to include the tips to create a bass note as well. Including the tips ensures that the 16th note rotation is not interrupted as well. Use the bass note with your fingertips that was introduced in Chapter 10, where the fingertip accent is moved over slightly from the edge of the pandeiro so that your ring and middle finger accent the drum. The goal is to make an open note like your thumb does.

Variation for choro/samba

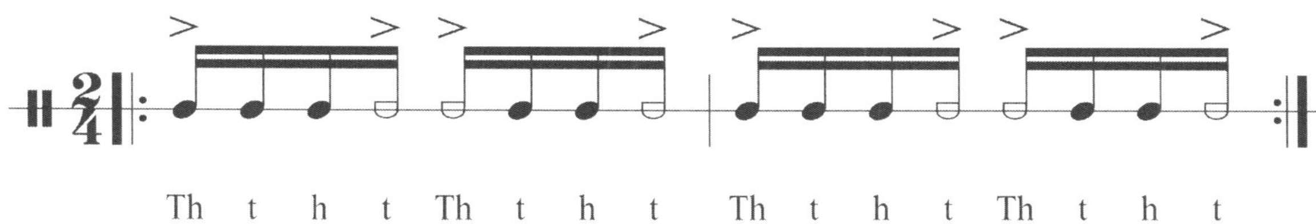

To begin to fill in with the pandeiro, the following examples will illustrate patterns that are similar to fills from a surdo drum.

Example 1

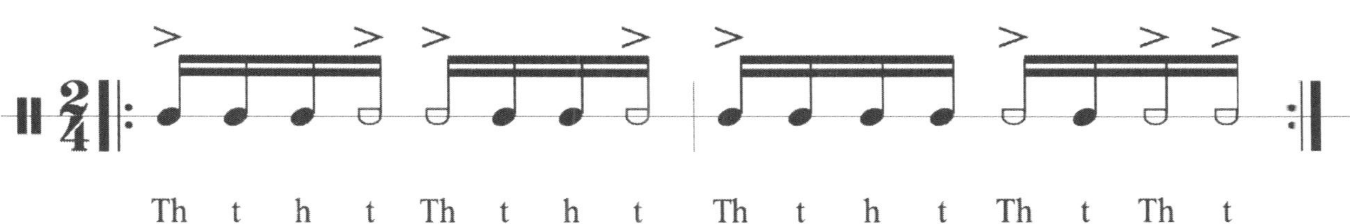

Example 2

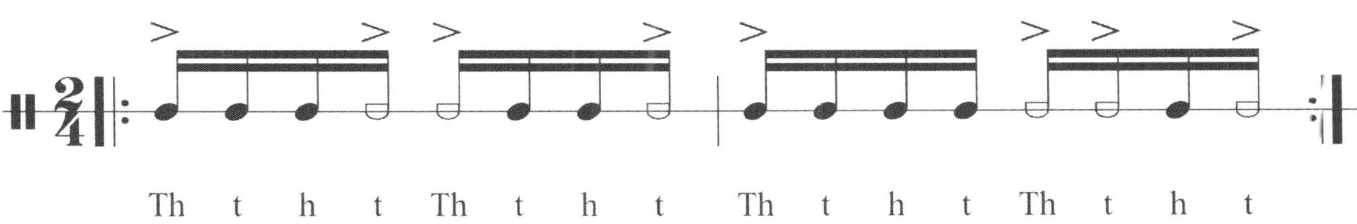

Example 3

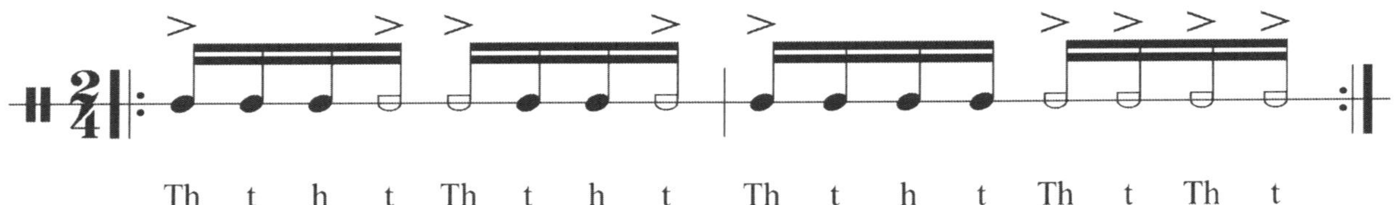

Example 4

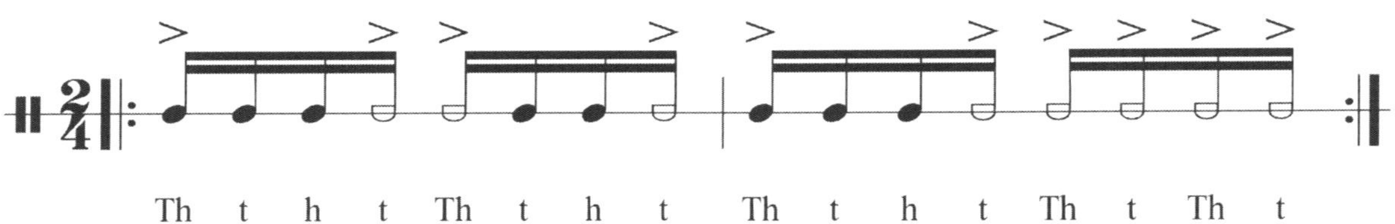

Example 5

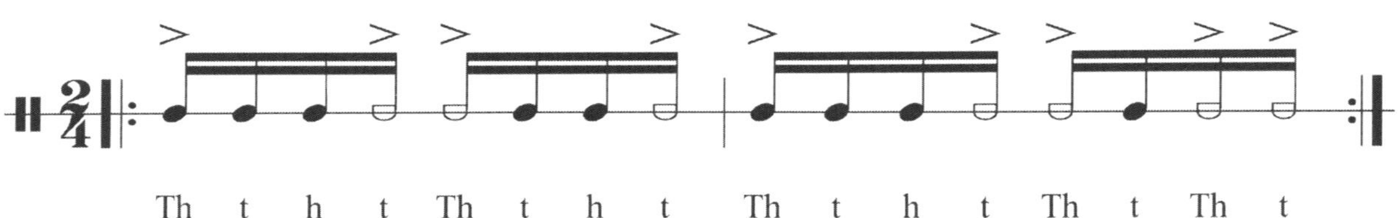

Example 6

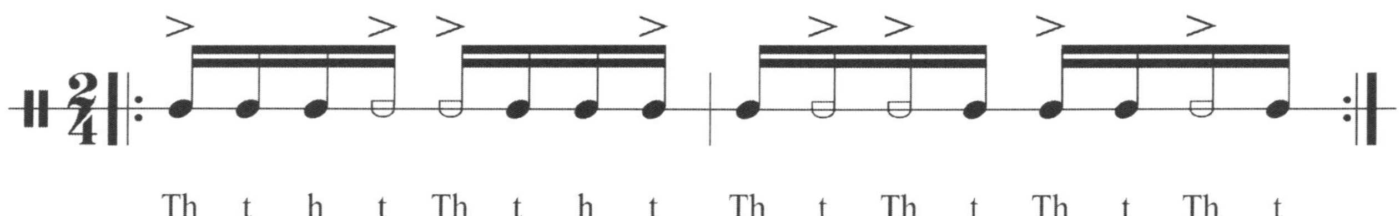

Example 7

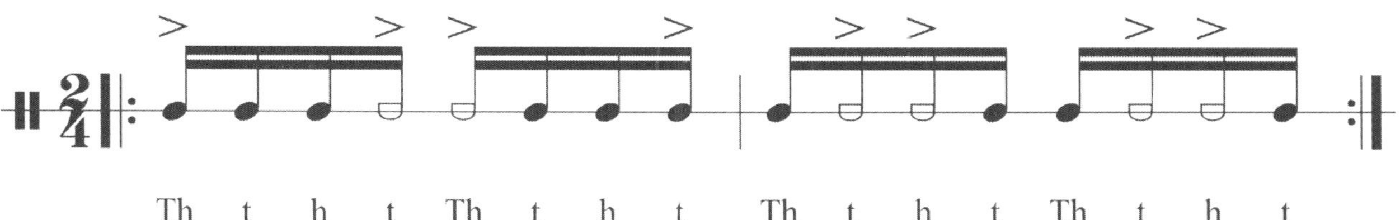

Example 8

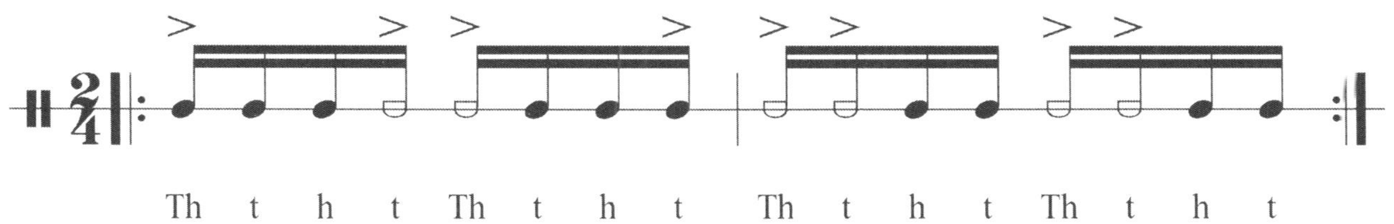

Example 10

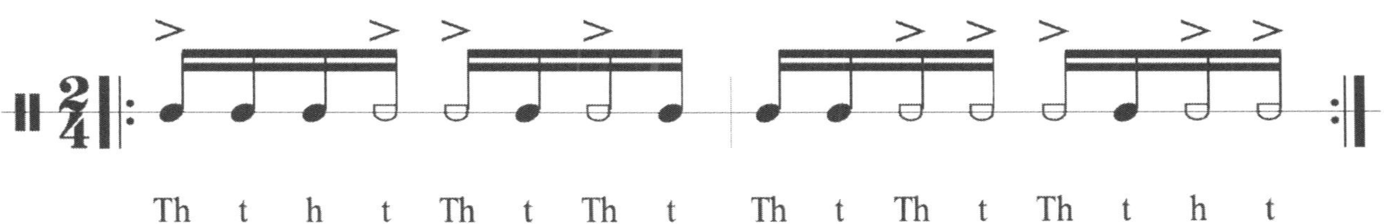

Example 11

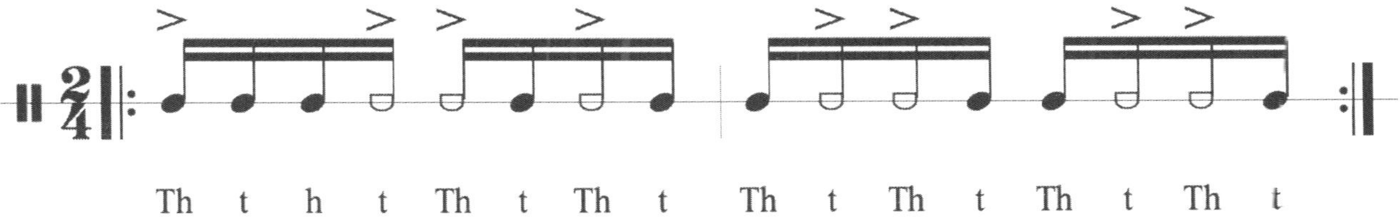

Chapter 16. Typical Endings for Samba or Choro (i.e. Jam Setting)

Written below are two cycles of samba on the top line and then the ending in the second line. Often at a jam session, (called a "roda" in Portuguese), a melodic player on the mandolin or clarinet for example, might initiate this phrase to signal the end of the song.

Example 1

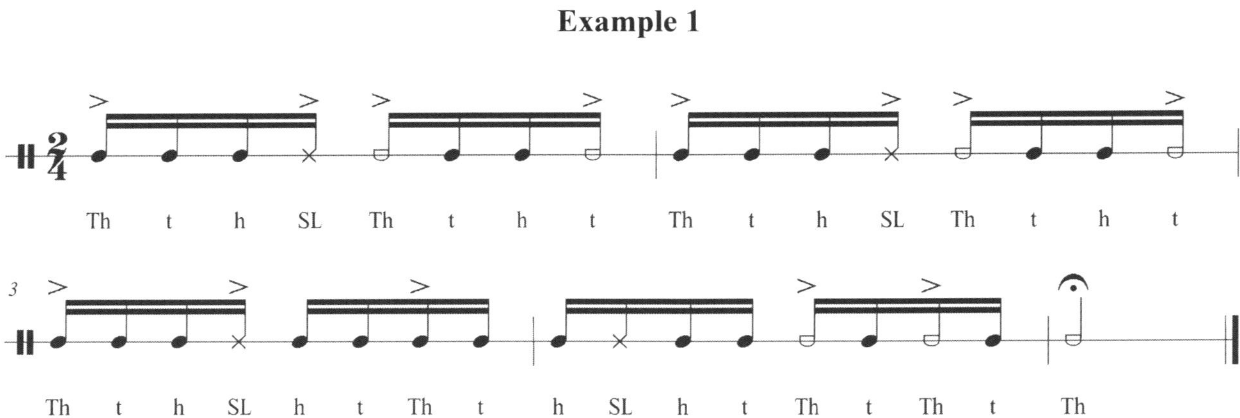

Example 2: This ending begins on the "e" of beat 1 on the second line.

Example 3: This ending starts in the last cycle of samba and is a short ending.

Example 4: This cycle ends on all upbeats.

Chapter 17. The Choro Ballad

In a slow-tempo choro ballad, the basic choro pattern is played but with almost metronomic 16th-note attention. In a ballad, the pandeiro's role is more about playing time evenly and consistently. To embellish the end of a phrase or section, there are some double time fills and phrasing that can be used but listening to examples is important to get a sense of doing this tastefully. Any fill traditionally should be something that won't interfere with the melody and is used more sparsely.

16th Note Rotation with basic choro pattern

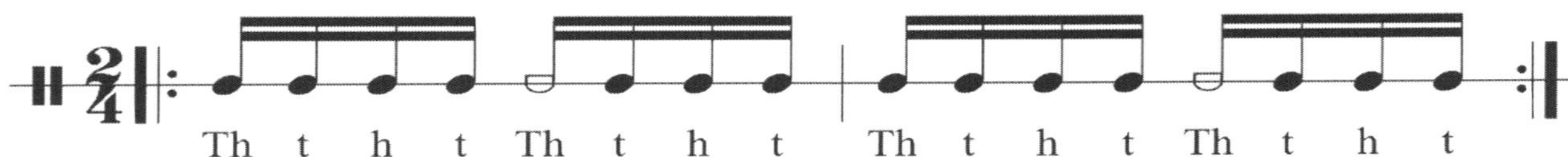

Example 1

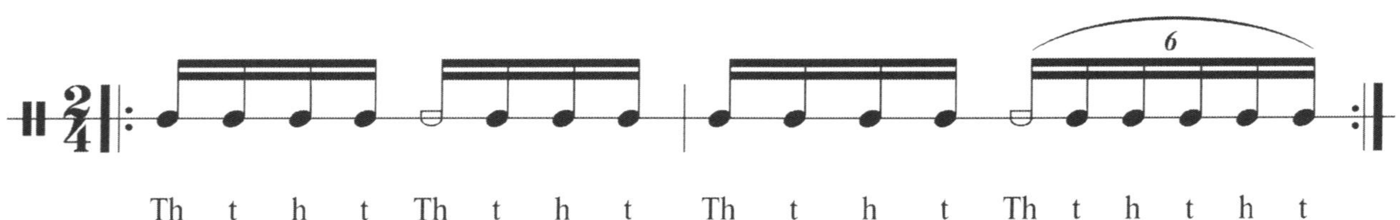

Example 2

Practice at a slow tempo and then play double time like this examble on beat 4.

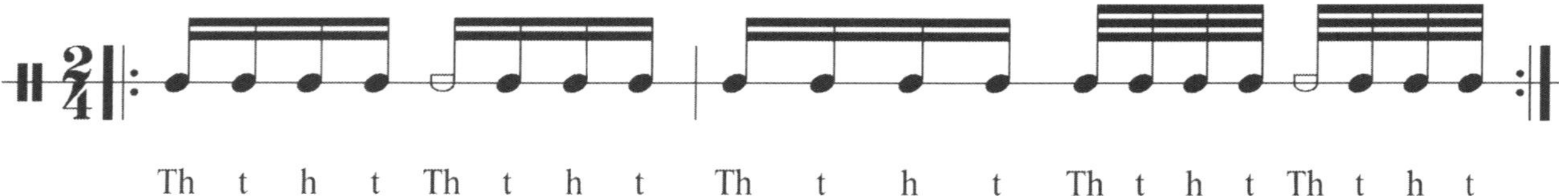

Example 3

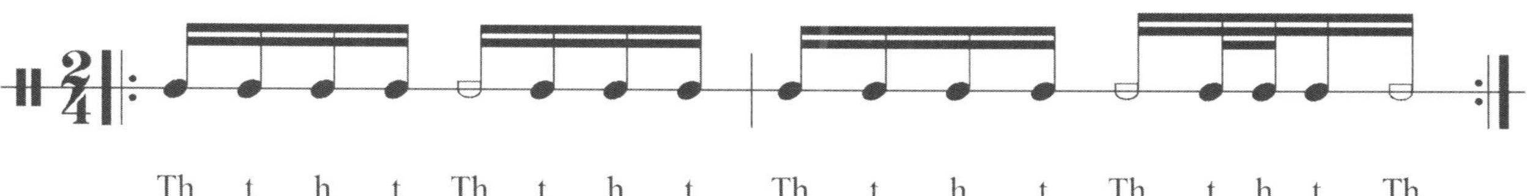

Example 4

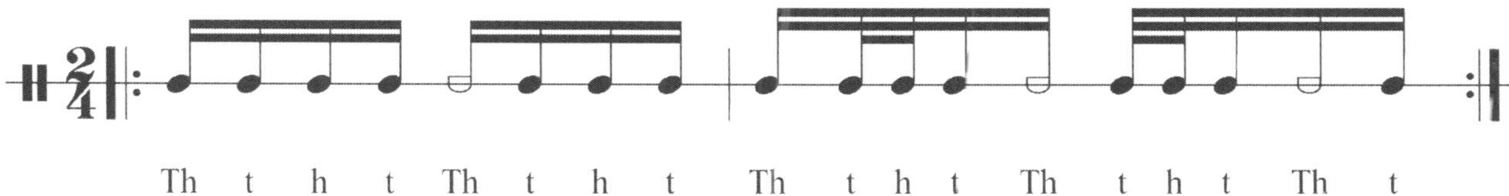

Choro Ballad Listening Suggestions

- *Ingênuo by Pixinguinha*
- *Mágoas by Jacob do Bandolim*
- *Choro Negro by Paulinho da Viola*

Chapter 18. The Brazilian Tamborim

What is a Tamborim?

The tamborim, which translates to "little drum," is a small frame drum. In samba schools, it's played mostly with a plastic head. For smaller ensembles or with acoustic instruments like choro or samba groups that play acoustically also known as "samba de raiz" a natural head can be used. Before the tamborim, the "caixeta" or wood block was used.

Depending on the style of music: bossa nova, samba, pagode or choro; the drum is played with a narrow thin stick called a baqueta. In samba schools, a nylon stick with small plastic rods/tines is used with 3, 5, 7, or many small plastic rods/tines making up the stick such as a "Baqueta de 7 Pontas" for example. In acoustic music or a smaller ensemble, the tamborim is usually played with the wooden baqueta. Sometimes a musician will play with their finger as well.

In the samba schools that perform during the Brazilian Carnaval, the tamborim section is extremely important and often consists of up to 100 players. Sometimes the tamborim section is referred to as the "horn section" because of the decorative patterns/designs or "desenhos" that are constantly played during a performance. Their role is to enliven the samba school. In the samba school playing the "tamborim ride" is known as the "tele-co-teco." If tamborim players are playing "virado" it is another pattern. "Virado" means turning in Portuguese. For utilizing the pandeiro we will focus on the "tele-co-teco."

The Tamborim Ride: Why It's Important

The traditional tamborim pattern in samba can vary quite a bit but is known as the "levada" or ride. It is a binary rhythm, meaning that there is a downbeat side and an upbeat side to this rhythm and it's a 2-bar pattern in either 2/4 or 4/4. The important thing to understand is whether the upbeat or downbeat side of the melody or phrase of a song is being played. It's very important to learn to play this pattern both ways.

The pattern is used and understood by all musicians playing the music. You will hear it referenced in every melodic instrument in some way. In addition, the cavaquinho (small string instrument) also plays this pattern/ride in choro and samba.

Once you know this pattern internally, you will just hear any change from an upbeat side to a downbeat side or know which side of the pattern is being played. The melody of the song will let you know if the "ride" is on the upbeat or downbeat side, and it can change throughout the song depending on how the musicians interpret it. When playing choro and with other musicians, take your cue from the guitar player and/or cavaquinho player as well as following the melody of the song being played.

A classic example is the famous samba, "Aquarela do Brasil" by Ary Barroso. The tamborim ride is used in the melody and is clearly starting on the downbeat side.

The following notation is for a tamborim played with a stick and muted with the finger on the back of the drum.
Drumstick = x; Finger closed =q; Finger open = h

Example 1

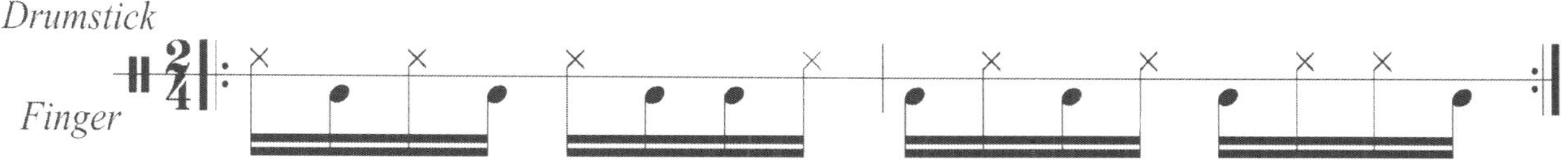

Example 2

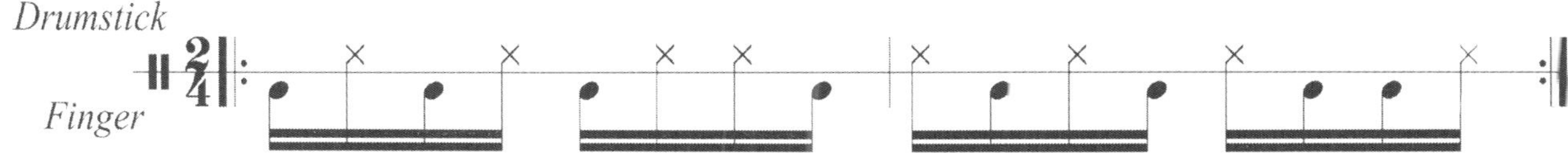

Learn it both ways and learn it comfortably both ways and apply it to the pandeiro.

Example 3

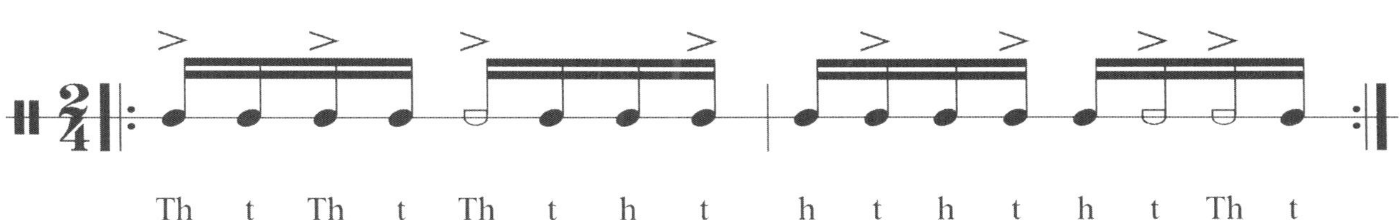

Example 4

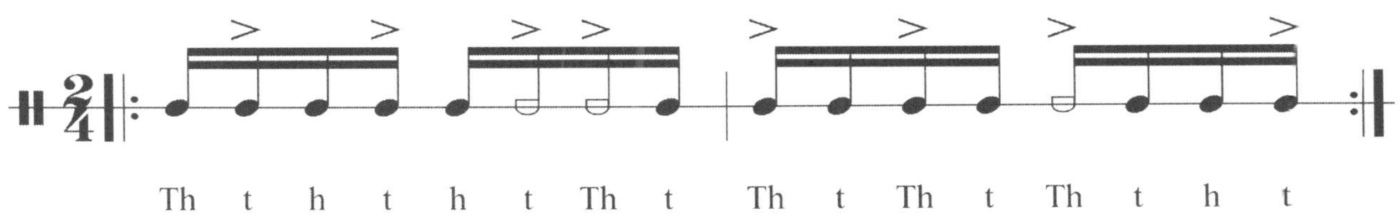

Example 5

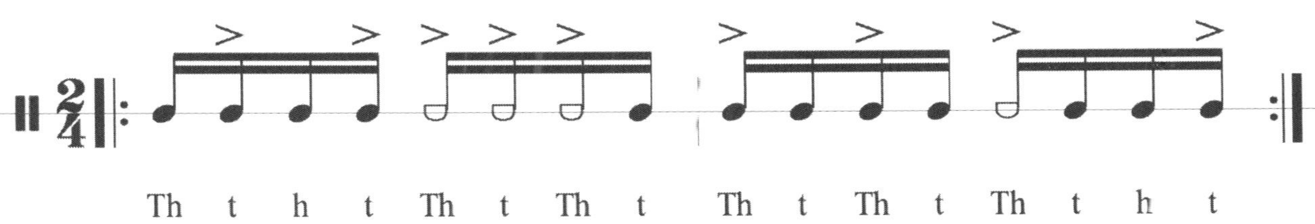

Chapter 19. Lundu

To better understand the evolution of maxixe, choro and samba we need to look back at rhythms such as the lundu and the habanera.

Lundu: The lundu evolved out of a connection to a circle dance from Angola, called the "Umbigada Angolana." African-influenced drums called "atabaques" (traditional drums) and handclaps were used as accompaniment. In the 18th century, before it became popular, the lundu had been banned in public.

It was re-introduced years later as a song style and was called a "canção" where it moved into the musical styles performed in the elite salons of Brazil and was even brought back to Portugal where it became popular there.

This European version of the lundu was accompanied by piano. Several styles of lundu were created such as the polca-lundu and the tango-lundu. Some historians believe the lundu was also influenced by the Fandango, which spread throughout Europe and the colonies in the mid-1700s.

Lundu Rhythm

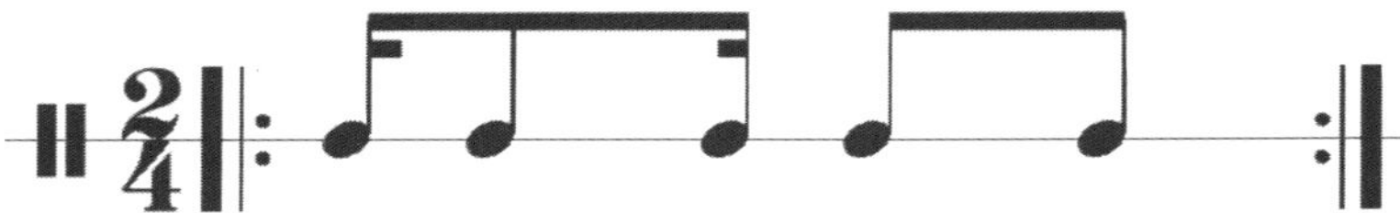

Lundu Listening Suggestions

- *Isto e Bom by Xisto Bahia*
- *Umbigada by author unknown*
- *Lundu da Marquesa de Santos by Villa Lobos*

Chapter 20. Maxixe and Tango Brasileiro

This is a rhythm and style of music dating back to the late 1800s. Maxixe is truly the first Brazilian music and became known later as part of the genre of choro. Maxixe is often referred to as "tango brasileiro" and was used by composers such as Ernesto Nazareth and Chiquinha de Gonzaga. Ernesto Nazareth referred to his maxixes as "tango brasileiros" because of the ill-reputation of the maxixe dance style which was a couple dance with the couple dancing very close together. At the time this was seen as indecent, not allowed publicly, and not for upper-class audiences.

While there were tango styles like the tango-habanera and possibly tango brasileiro in popularity in Brazil nearly 10 years before it became popular in Argentina, the confusion about the two styles came from the reputation.

Chiquinha Gonzaga previewed a maxixe called "O Gaucho" also titled "Dança do Corte Jaca" which debuted in 1895. While it was initially seen as scandalous, became popular among all the classes due to a small group of upper-class women of "high society" who were the "influencers" of the day and made it fashionable.

"O Gaucho" or "Dança do Corte Jaca" was not the first maxixe written but the maxixe became very popular in Paris and abroad through a Brazilian dancer, Duque, who was living in Paris. Duque was also responsible for bringing the great composer Pixinguinha to Paris and spreading Brazil's dances and music abroad to salons in Europe, America, and back in Brazil.

Up until this point in time, dancers like Duque would travel to Paris and pick up the latest dances for the season of balls and events abroad before then bringing them back to Brazil.

Maxixe however, was imported to Europe and the world directly from Brazil as a Brazilian musical style and dance, thus putting Brazil on the "cultural" map internationally. The maxixe became fashionable as a dance in the U.S. and traveled as far as the former Soviet Union.

Pixinguinha wrote choros, maxixes, polcas, sambas and many different styles of music. His band "Os Oito Batutas," music and time in Paris was a huge influence and furthered the maxixe and choro to the world at large, so much so that he was celebrated as a national hero when he returned to Brazil.

Some of the major influences for the maxixe are from the polka/polca, the African-based rhythm of lundu and the Spanish habanera. There were many styles of tango based on the habanera and milonga rhythms as well as many variations of polca as well. Both Chiquinha de Gonzaga and Ernesto Nazareth were influential piano players and the left hand in their compositions will showcase how these rhythms started to integrate into choro creating the maxixe and creating polca styles.

Habanera Rhythm

Habanera Rhythm 2 or variation

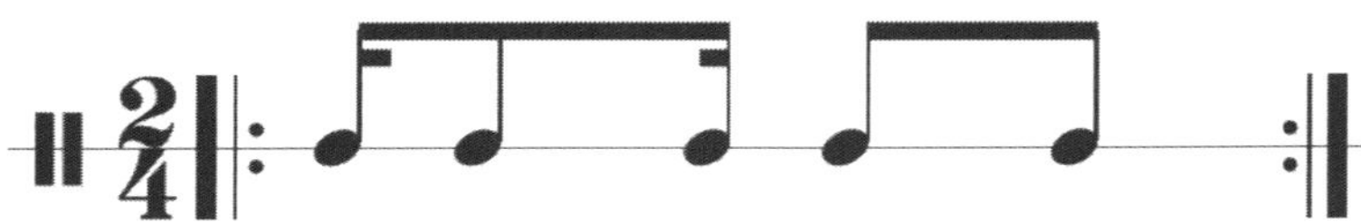

Maxixe pattern often played by melody line

Example 1: Basic maxixe pattern exercise accenting only the bass notes

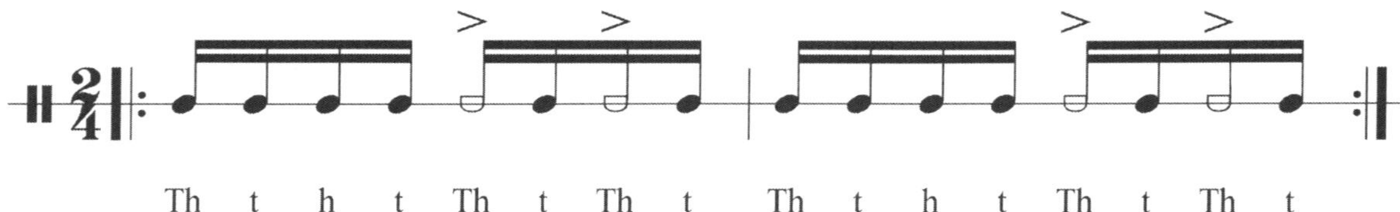

Example 2: With the habanera influence, include the accent on the "a" of beat 1, leading into beat 2.

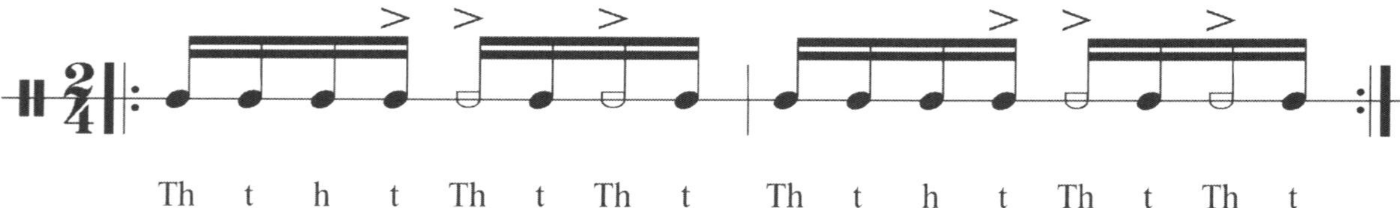

Example 3: Some maxixe patterns remind the listener of a northeastern baião rhythm but still are a maxixe. This is also because of the habanera influence.

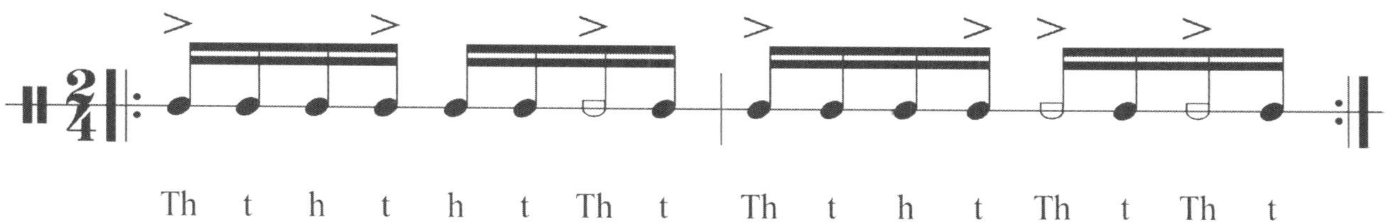

Example 4: To accent the "e" of beat 1, some variations add a trill or roll on the drum.

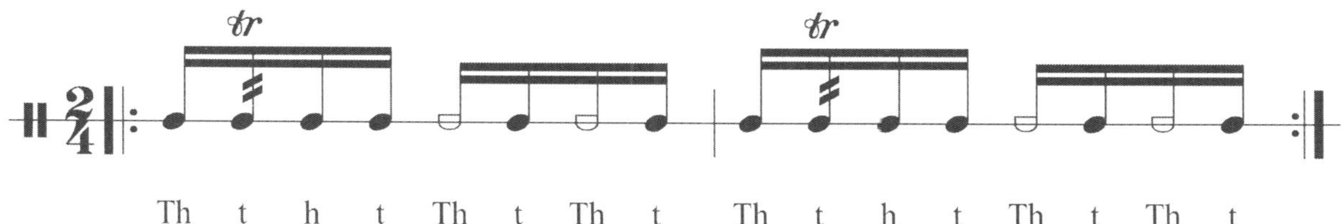

Example 5

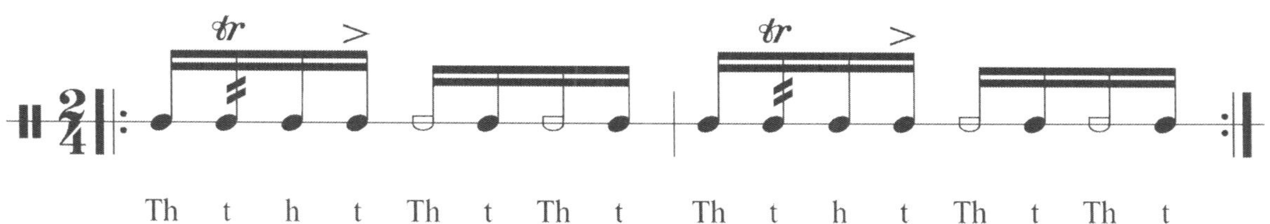

Example 6

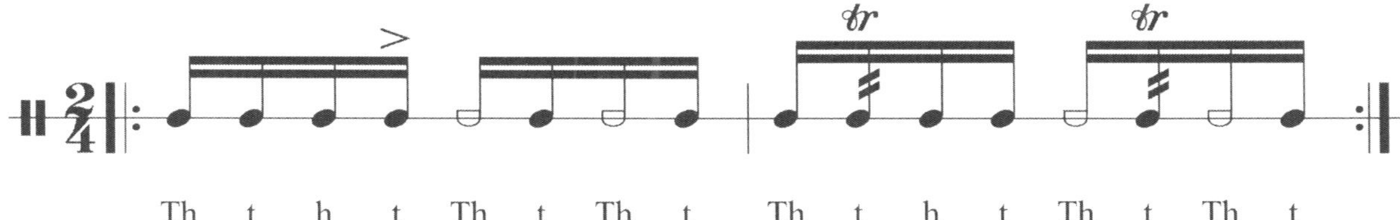

Example 7

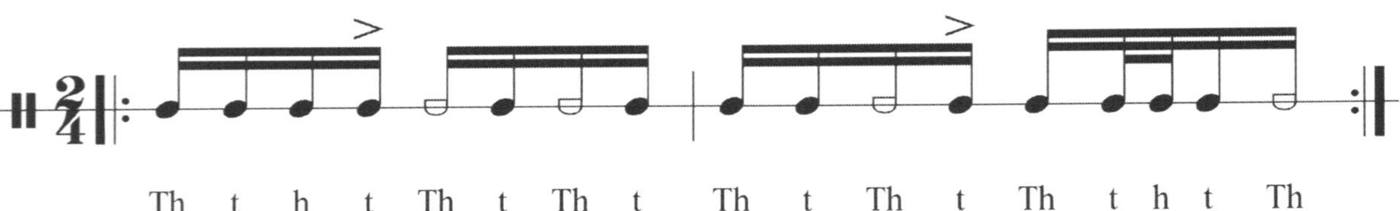

Maxixe Listening Suggestions

- *Odeon by Ernesto Nazareth (*called a "Tango Brasileiro")*
- *Myosotis by Ernesto Nazareth*
- *Jura by Sinho (originally a maxixe and now played as a samba)*
- *Gaucho/Dança de Corta Jaca by Chiquinha Gonzaga*
- *Sultana by Chiquinha Gonzaga*
- *Atraënte by Ernesto Nazareth*
- *Ali Babá by Henrique Alves de Mesquita ** Tango Habanera*

Chapter 21. Polca

The polca or polka is a style of music originating from Europe, specifically in Bohemia also known as Czechoslovakia (now the Czech Republic). Polka or polca as it's spelled in Portuguese became popular in the mid 1840s throughout Brazil, introduced through European culture and music evolving with its own Brazilian flare into several variations and styles of Brazilian polca. The Brazilian musical stye of maxixe evolved with large influence of both the polca and Afro-Brazilian lundu. There are several variations of the polca in Brazil such as the polca-militar, polca-lundu, polca-choro, etc.

Isn't a Polca just a Polca?

The straight feel of a Brazilian basic polca is just like the European polka. However, what is important, is that because of the European music being played in Brazil, composers would start to compose Brazilian polcas with a few bars in the melody of a particular swing that was influenced by the African or African-Brazilian musical styles such as: lundu, batuque, or the Spanish habanera. The Brazilian polca started to incorporate elements of an inflection or "swing" from these rhythmic influences. Most polcas in a choro format are played like a maxixe or lean to that style. For the pandeiro the maxixe and some polca rhythm fill in the 16th notes instead of 8th notes. Some polcas are more straight like a European polka, some are more filled in with 16th notes and one leans towards a northeastern swing of a baiao or côco.

Example 1 Basic Polca Rhythm

Below are examples of polca fills or polca embellishments but mostly to play polca depending on the melody and rhythm section would be to play it as a maxixe. (See previous chapter.)

Example 2

Th t Th t Th t h t Th

Example 3

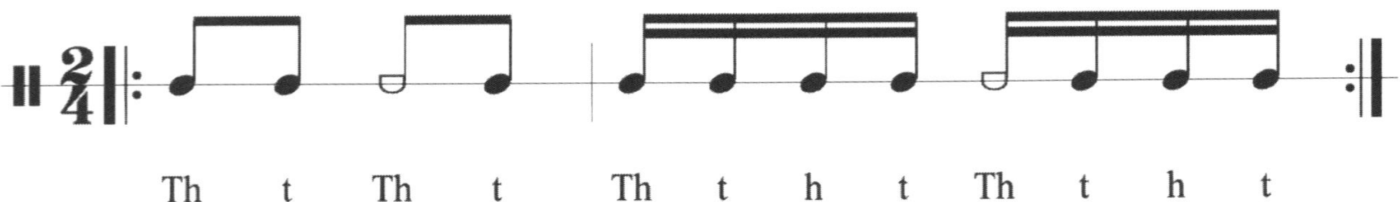

Example 4

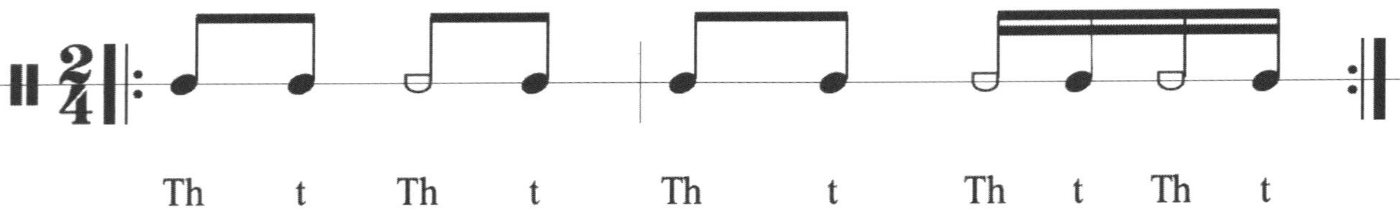

Polca Listening Suggestions

- *Marreco Quer Agua by Pixinguinha*
- *Tô Fraco by Pixinguinha*
- *Apanhai-Te Cavaquinho by Ernesto Nazareth*
- *Polca em Sol by Mario Álvares-Conceição*

Chapter 22. Marcha

Marcha, which means, "march" in Portuguese, can also be referred to as a "marchiña" which means "little march." Marcha lenta or frevo lento were popular during the turn of the 20th century and evolved out of clubs and parade groups called Carnavalescos. Carnavalescos were groups that paraded in Carnaval and still exist today. The structure of Carnavlescos was the precursor to the samba schools or blocos. Each "Carnavalesco" was accompanied by a full and complete marching band which played music with horns, clarinet, flutes, piccolo and percussion with primarily marching rhythms until the late 1930s. It was in the following decade that samba rhythms started to emerge in parading groups or blocos. Similar to the samba schools, the marching rhythm and election of a king and queen were loose and secular interpretations of the royal military bands and court. The below marcha rhythms evoke the pattern a snare drum would play.

Example 1

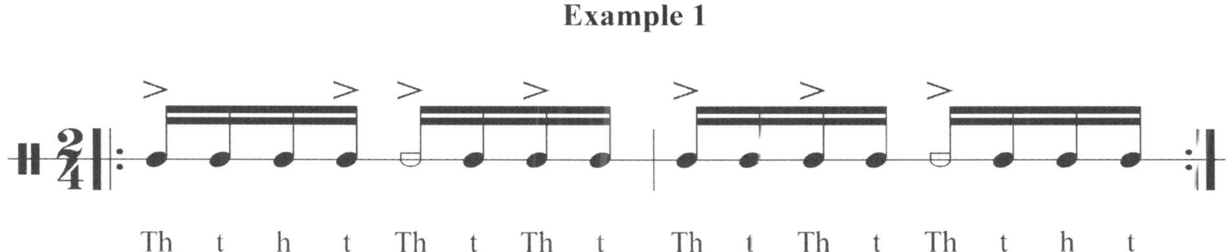

Example 2: Marcha Antigo *(old march)*

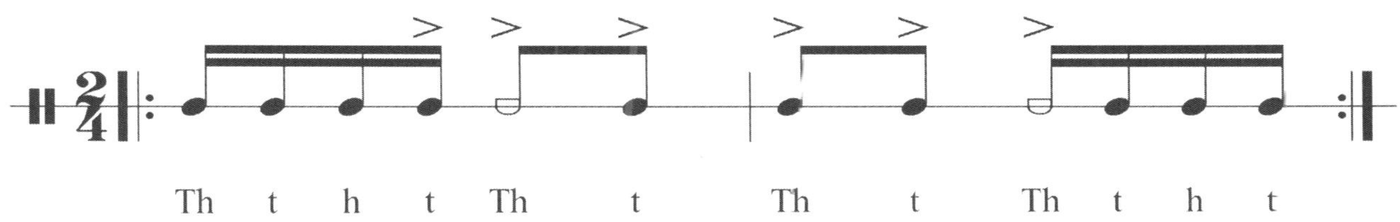

Example 3: Additional march variation considered a "*marcha lenta*" *(slow march)*

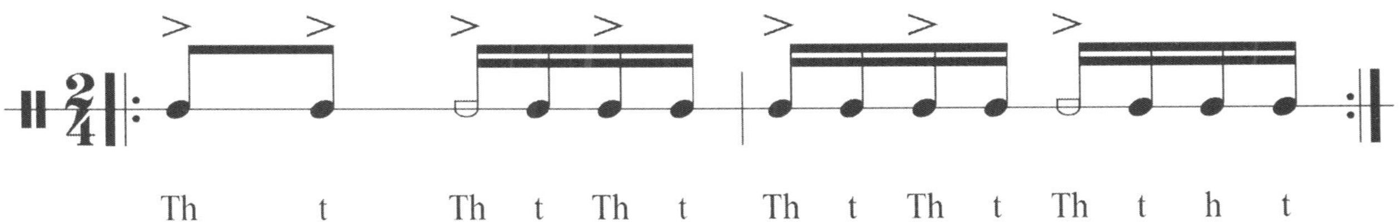

Example 4

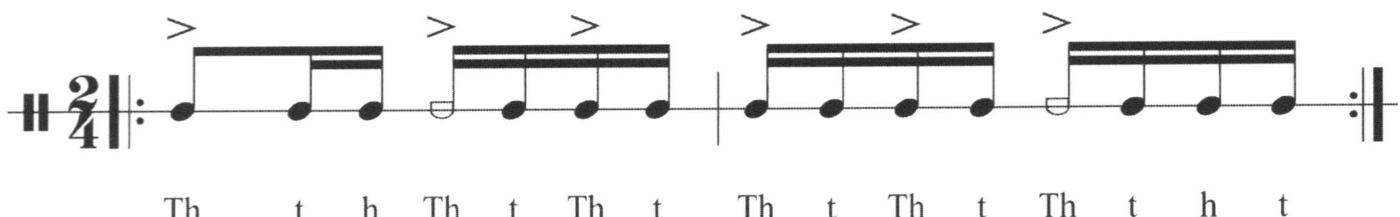

Example 5

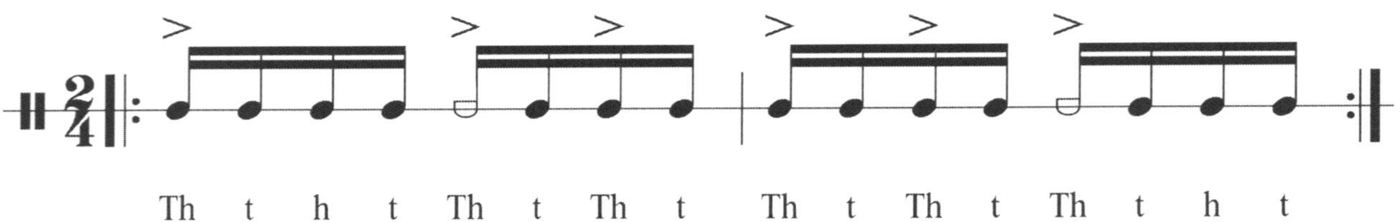

Example 6

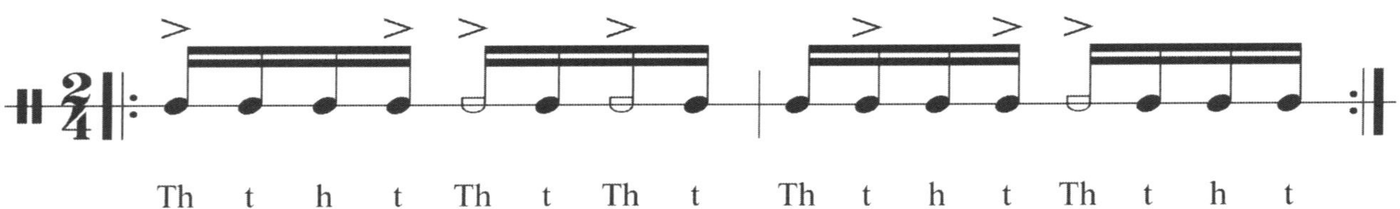

Example 7

Example 8

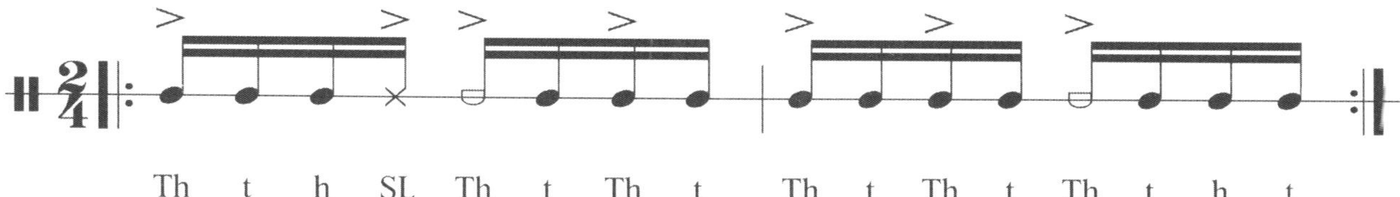

Example 9

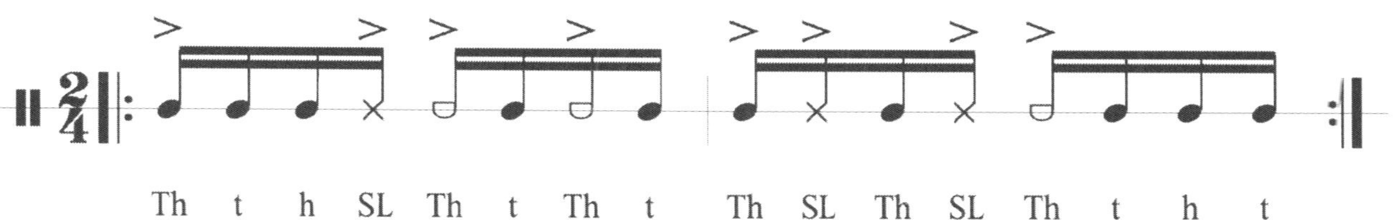

Example 10

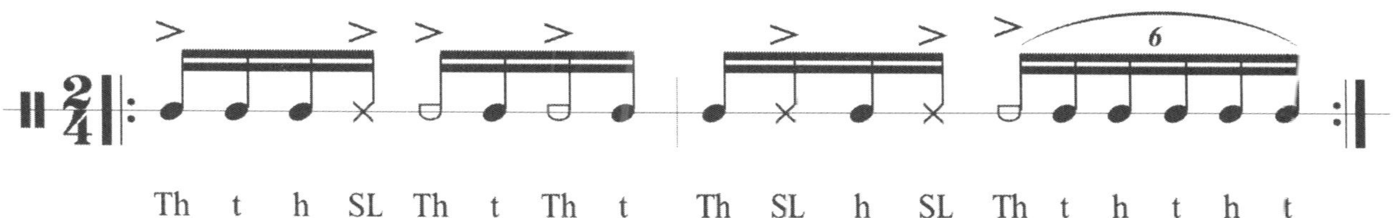

Example 11

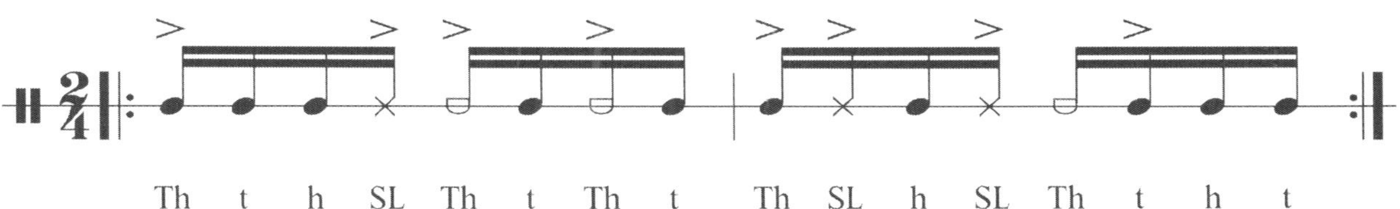

Example 12

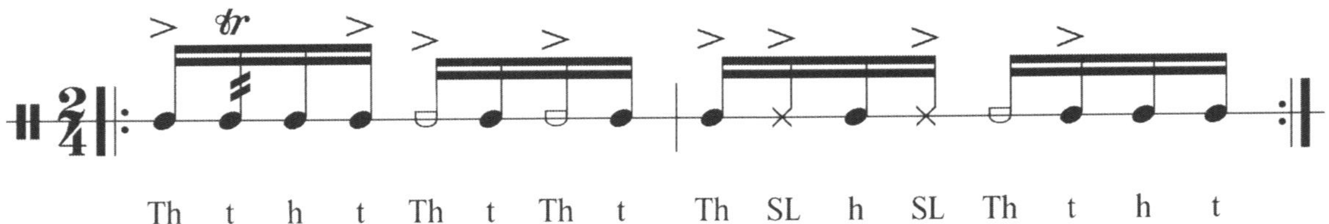

Example 13: Reminder that the "tr" is a "*trill*" or "*roll.*"

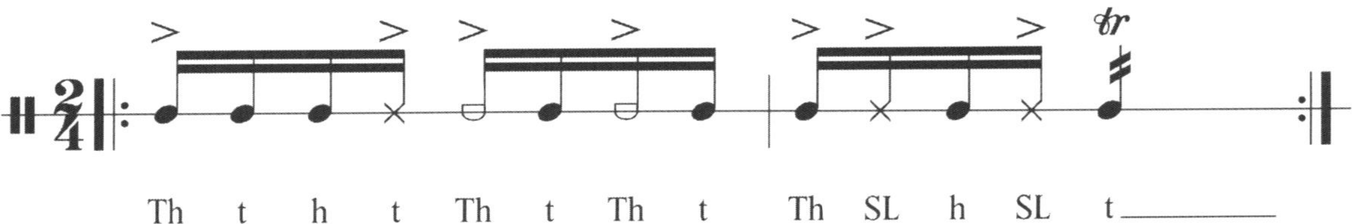

Marcha Listening Suggestions

- *Ó Abre Alas by Chiquinha Gonzaga*
- *Marcha dos Marinheiros by Raphael Rabello*
- *Flor de Abacate by Alvaro Sandim*

Chapter 23. Northeastern Brazilian Rhythms: Baião

The most popular Northeastern music in Brazil is called forró. A "forró" describes a dance, event, party, and/or style of music. June marks the month of two feast days and celebrations that celebrate with music called, "Festa de São João" and "Festa Juneenah" and can center on the agricultural harvest, which comes during Brazil's colder months or winter.

There are many misconceptions about what the origin of the word forró means. One theory is that Brazilians were trying to say in English "for all" to invite American GIs to local dancehall events and it sounded instead like the word "forró." Many American GIs were stationed in Brazil during WWII. Another theory that supersedes the prior one, is the word originates from a slang word, "forrobodó" which means a get-together and was commonly used in the 1940s.

Within forró music there are several musical styles such as: côco, baião, xaxado, xote, ciranda and a myriad of other rhythms as well. Baião is a contemporary rhythm that defines the forró dance music. Côco is very similar but has more variations, styles, and rhythms such as côco de congada or côco embolada. Côco in origin is a rhythm with many kinds of variations. Côco is a dance and one form known as "côco de roda" means it is danced in a circle. Its origins are a mix of African and Indigenous Brazilian influence. Côco and baião rhythms as well as xaxado, are felt in the same grouping of 3 beats, 3 beats, and 2 beats (or 3:3:2). The wide-spread popularity of forró and baião is credited largely to Luiz Gonzaga, a great composer and musician from Pernambuco which is in Northeastern Brazil.

Please note that there are extensive rhythm repertoires for each of these musical styles and rhythmic patterns, but for the purpose of this instructional manual as a beginning guide, we are going to teach only the basic rhythms and improvisations.

The pandeiro copies the rhythms of the zabumba: a two-sided drum played with a mallet in one hand and a small wooden stick on the other. It's important to understand that the slaps and open tones mimic the zabumba. The thin stick plays the upbeat on the plastic side of the drum and the open notes are playing the bass tones from the mallet side. The thin stick is called a "bacalhãu."

In addition, the xaxado, côco and baião rhythms are very similar in that they are felt in a 3:3:2 beat context with different accents marked depending on the rhythm. But all three are used as variations of each other. Because of the history and passing of oral tradition, some people in varying regions will call a baião a côco or vice versa. Some côco patterns are felt as a 2-bar pattern with the second half being a variation on the first.

Within forró musical styles, you might hear a zabumba player use licks for xaxado, côco and baião within the same song, because they are emphasizing different bass notes and most importantly embellishing the melody of the song and hearing where the accents fall.

Below are three ways to play a baião on the pandeiro. Different ways to organize hand movements are used to play the pattern with subsequent variations.

- Example #1 is traditional and starts with the thumb.
- Example #2 is also starting on the thumb.
- Example #3 starts with the tips.

Example 1: Traditional baião pattern starting with thumbs. This is a more traditional way of playing, however the fingering is awkward because of the heel-to-thumb movement, yet it is widely used.

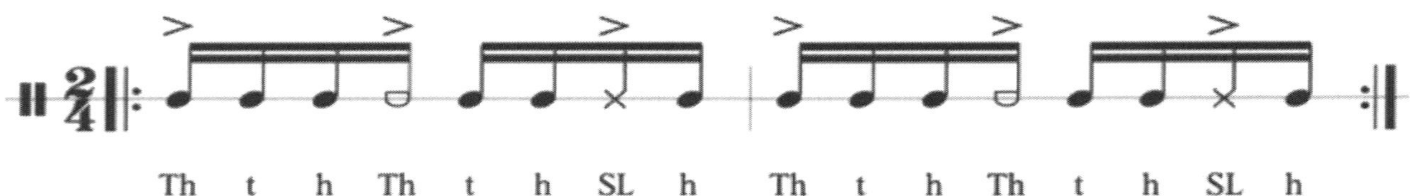

Th t h Th t h SL h Th t h Th t h SL h

Example 2: Traditional baião rhythm starting on thumbs but played in a more contemporary way to accommodate 16th note rotation and adding a thumb-slap.

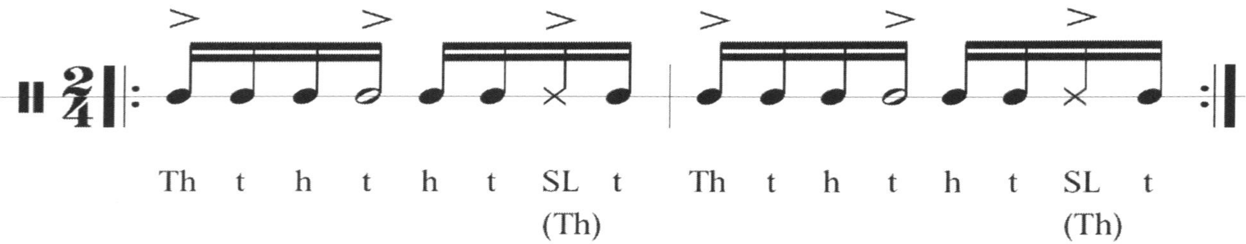

Th t h t h t SL t Th t h t h t SL t
(Th) (Th)

Example 2a: The same baião pattern but starting with the fingertips with constant 16th note rotation in the left hand.

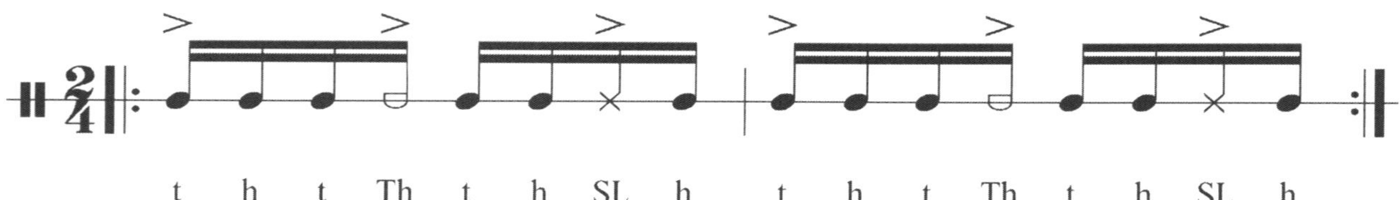

t h t Th t h SL h t h t Th t h SL h

Baião Variations

Example 1: Baião variation starting with the thumb

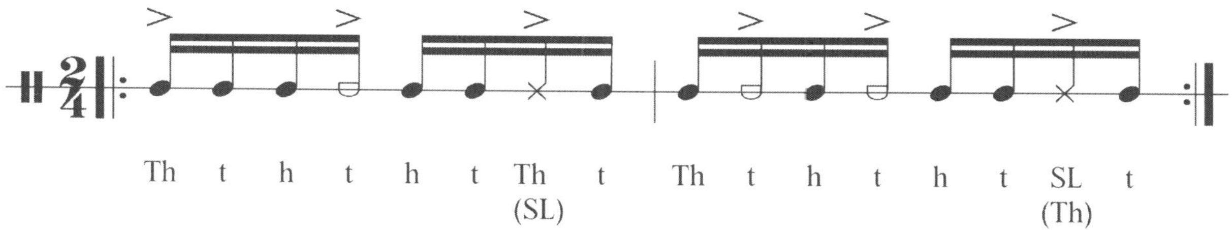

Example 1a: Baião variation starting with fingertips

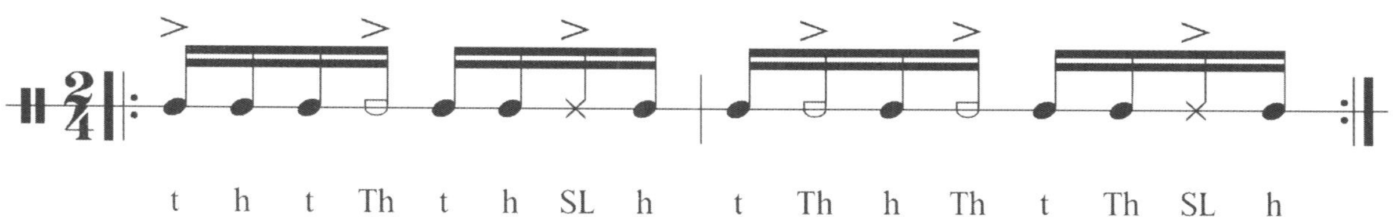

Example 2: Baião variation #2 starting with the thumb

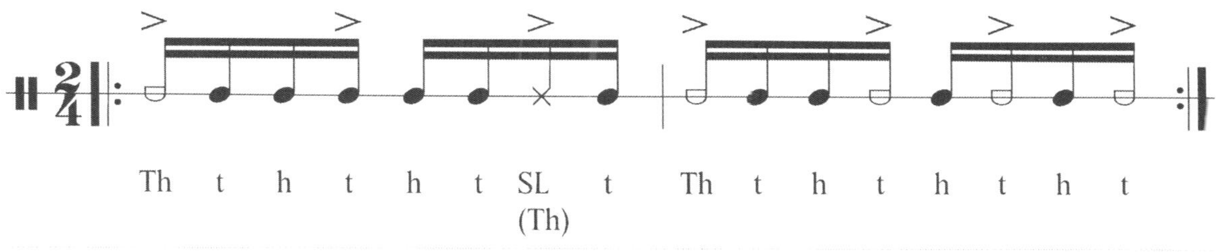

Example 2a: Baião variation #2 but starting with fingertips

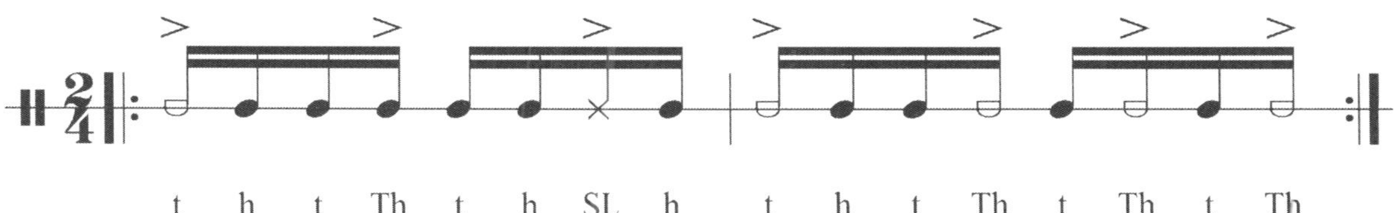

Example 3: Baião variation #3 starting on thumb

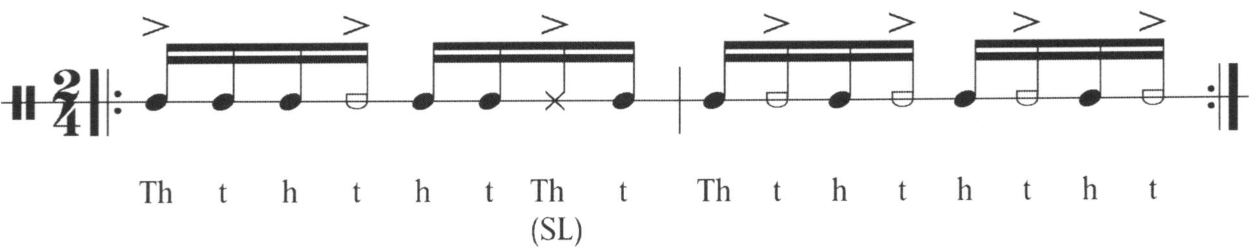

Example 3a: Baião variation #3a but starting with fingertips

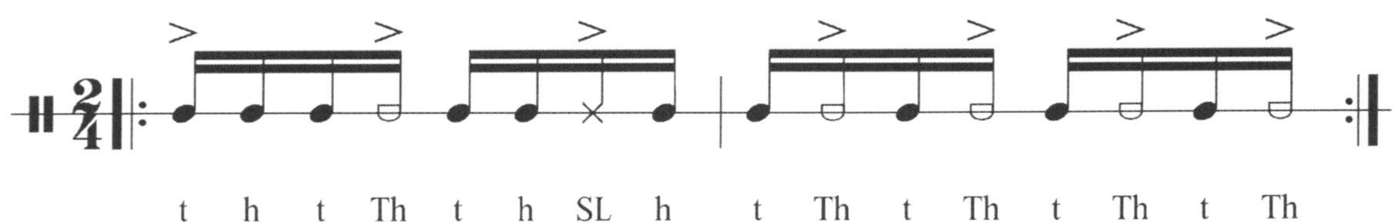

Example 4: Traditional baião rhythm starting on thumbs but played in a more contemporary way to accommodate 16th note rotation and adding a thumb-slap.

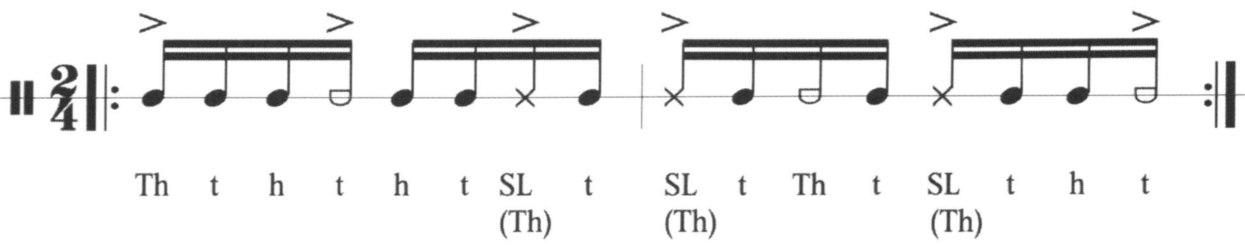

Example 4a: Baião variation #4 but starting with fingertips

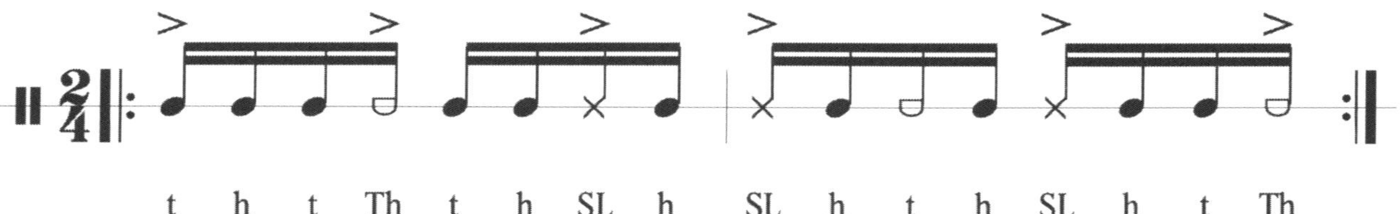

Example 5 Baião variation #5 starting on thumb

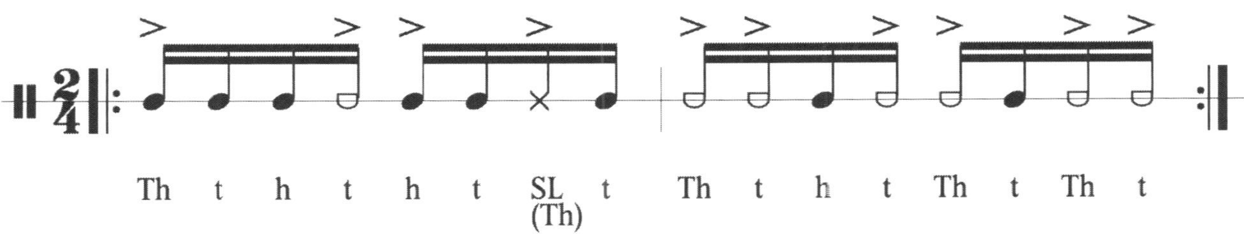

Example 5a: Baião variation #5 but starting with fingertips

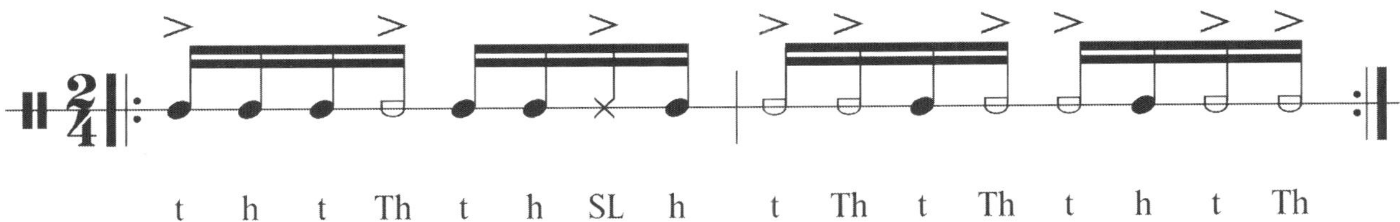

Example 6: Baião variation #6 starting on thumb

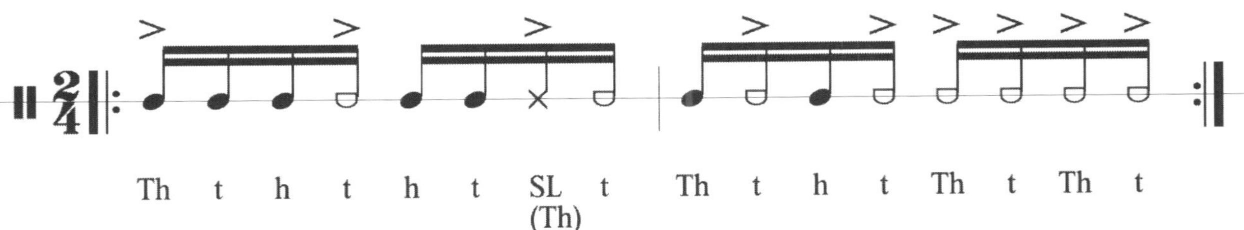

Example 6a: Baião variation #6 but starting with fingertips

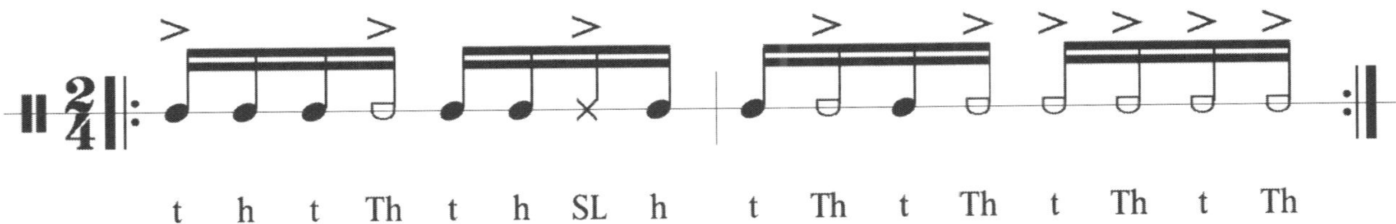

Baião Listening Suggestions

- *Baião by Luiz Gonzaga*
- *Ponteio by Edu Lobo*
- *Forró em Limoeiro by Jackson Do Pandeiro*
- *Etá Baião by Jackson do Pandeiro*

Chapter 24. Northeastern Brazilian Rhythms: Côco

Côco is a rhythm that falls under the forró repertoire. There are several musical styles and variations within côco. This book will not explore the vast and complex history but focus on a few of the most common styles as they relate to forró. One popular variation is the côco embolada which is performed between two performers in an improvised kind of vocal or rap battle. The improvised rhyming and metered stanzas are thrown back and forth between two vocalists who generally play pandeiros in a kind of "battle" in 2/4 time emphasizing the 3:3:2 rhythm. "Embolada" is a slang word that means "to entangle or entangling" and refers to the wordplay done in fast "machine-gun" style banter.

The name "coco" (Portuguese for "coconut") is a common Northeastern Brazilian slang for head, referring to the fact that song lyrics are often improvised.

In terms of forró, côco, baião and xaxado are elements that work with the 2/4 meter and 3:3:2 rhythm with accents on different areas. In côco the open beat "1" is determined by the lyrics and how they fall or are accented but in one song there can be both references to côco or baião which generally accents beat 2. Some songs also accent both beats. It's important to listen to the music and get familiar with it.

****Note: Slaps are generally "on the tips" side of things unless emphasized as a thumb slap.***

Example 1: Traditional côco pattern starting with thumbs

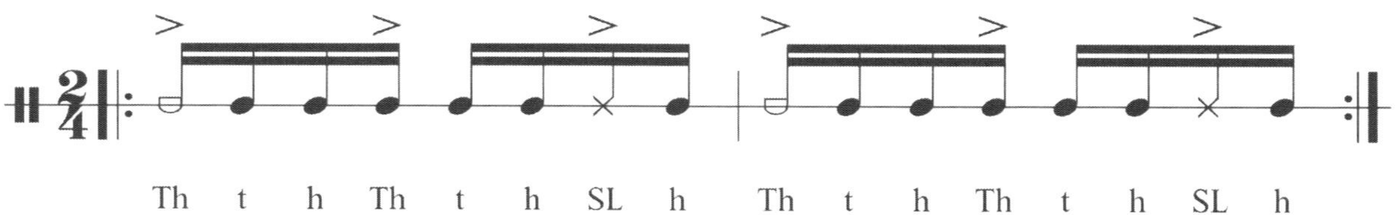

Example 2: Côco rhythm starting on thumbs but played in a more modern way to accommodate 16th note rotation. The slap is done with the thumb in the middle of the drum.

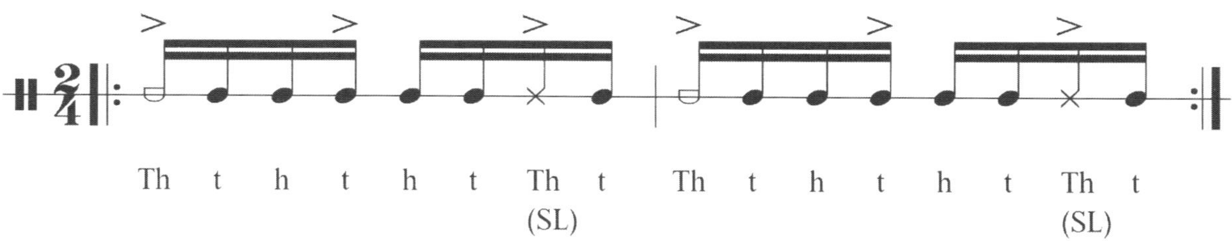

Note: Just like the baião pages, you can also start these rhythms with your tips.

Example 2a: Côco rhythm starting on tips but played in a more modern way to accommodate 16th note rotation. Slaps are on the "tip" side or replace where you would hit with tips.

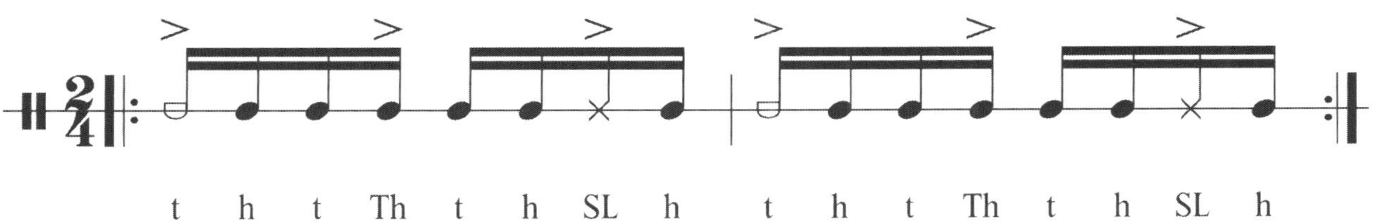

Example 3: Côco rhythm variation starting on thumbs.

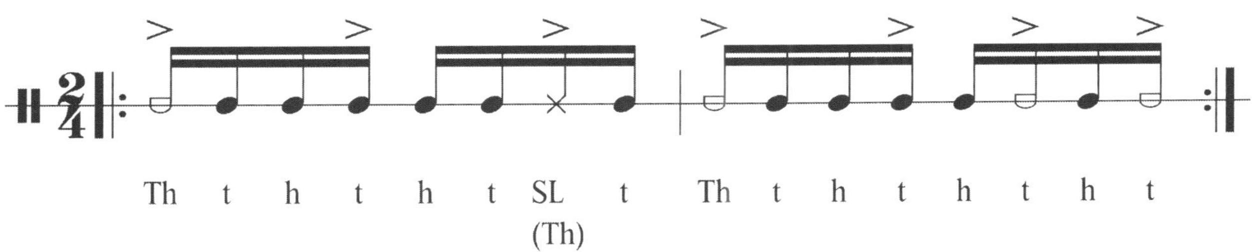

Example 3a: The same côco rhythm variation as played above but starting on tips.

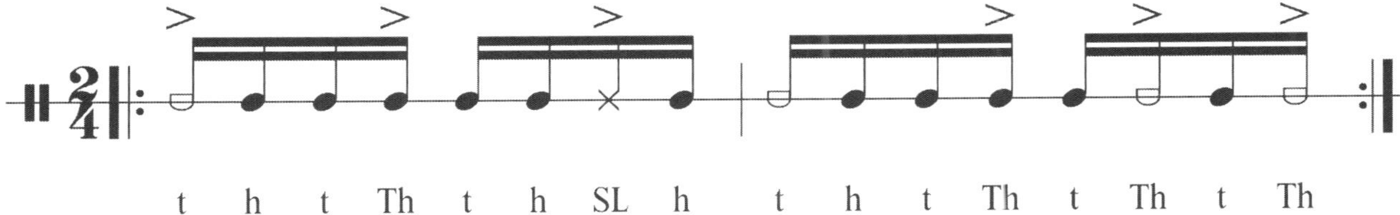

Example 4: The last note in the system, the "a" of 4 with a slash across, is to show an open tip but less accented in open tone than beat 1 for example.

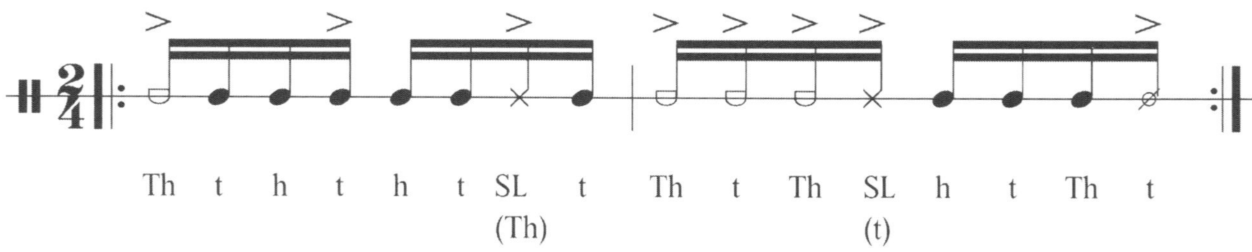

Example 4: Côco rhythm as played above but starting on tips. The last note in the system, the "a" of 4 with a slash across, is to show an open tip but less accented in open tone than beat 1 for example.

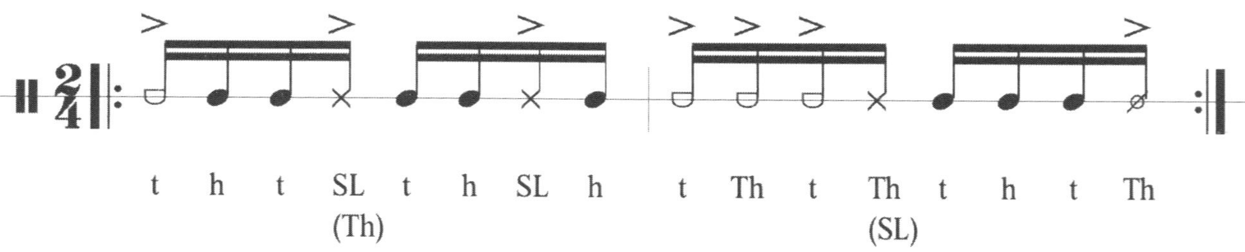

Example 5: Côco rhythm variation starting on thumbs.

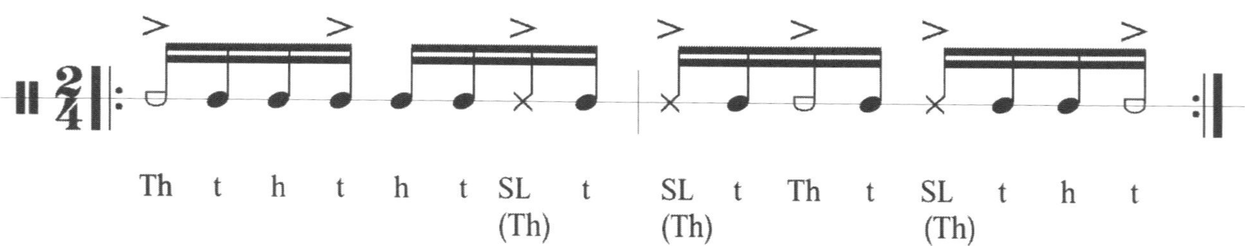

Example 5a: The same côco rhythm variation as played above but starting on tips.

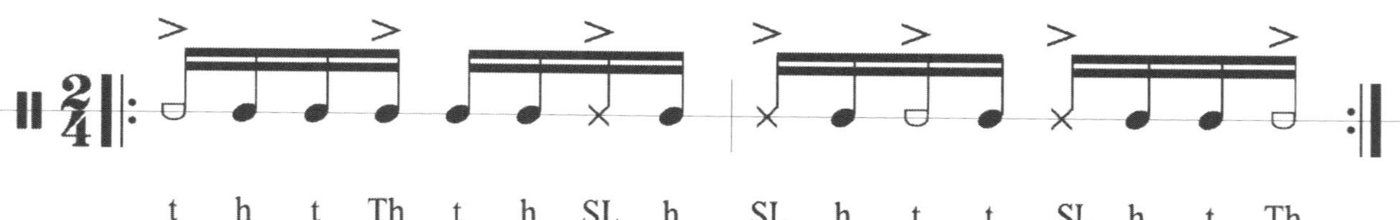

Example 6: Côco congada starting on thumbs.

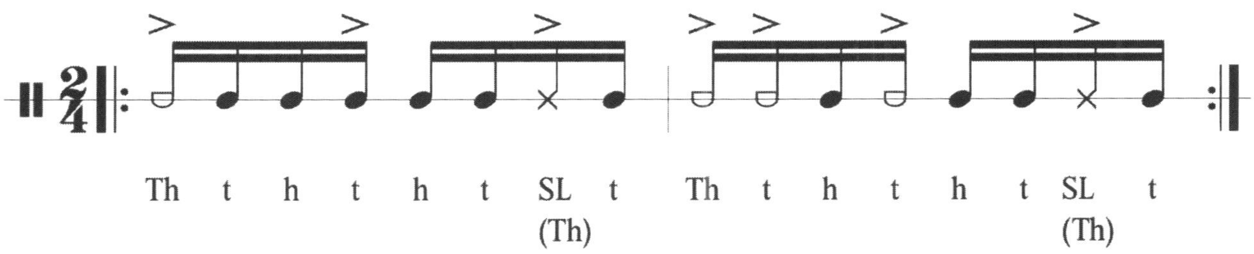

Example 6a: Côco congada starting with tips.

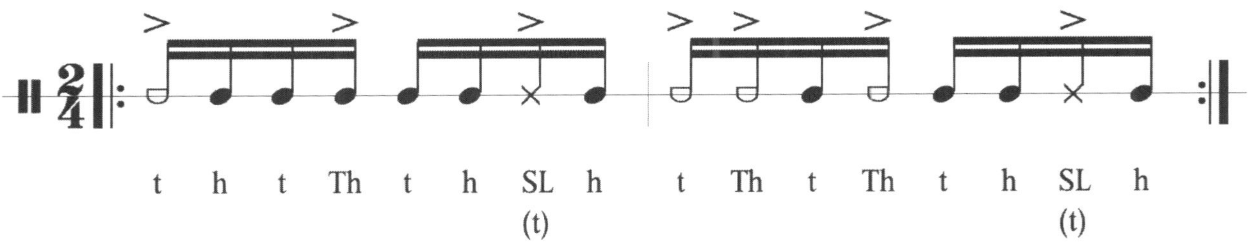

Côco Listening Suggestions

- *Côco do Norte by Jackson do Pandeiro*
- *Que Nim Jiló by Luiz Gonzaga*
- *Magdalena by Elba Ramalho & Sergio Mendez*
- *Asa Branca by Luiz Gonzaga*
- *Vovó Álaide by Cascabulho*

Chapter 25. Northeastern Brazilian Rhythms: Xaxado

Xaxado is a dance and stepping pattern from the 19th century and originates in the state of Pernambuco and the dry region known as the Sertão. The origins of xaxado are complex with some historians stating that it is from Portugal while others claim its roots are Indigenous. The dance resembles an indigenous movement, and the name is connected to the word "xaxar" which involves harvesting beans from the area.

Xaxado is also an onomatopoeic word that sounds like the leather sandals of peasants and farmers stepping on a sandy floor. It's often performed in folkloric groups with specific vocal songs and sticks or rifles used to hit the ground to represent the battles of the "Cangaceiros" or outlaws of the time. Xaxado historically has been performed by men and movements represent the rituals of harvest. In a contemporary use, it's played on the zabumba and part of the forró repertoire. It is also a variation pattern for baião or côco rhythms as all three have a similar syncopation of grouping and accenting around a 3:3:2 beat formation.

- Example #1 is traditional and starts with the thumb.
- Example #2 is also starting on the thumb.
- Example #3 starts with the tips.

Different ways to organize hand movements are used to play the pattern and subsequent variations.

Xaxado Basic Pattern

Traditional xaxado pattern starting with thumbs. This is a more traditional way of playing, however the fingering is awkward because of the heel-to-thumb movement yet it is widely used.

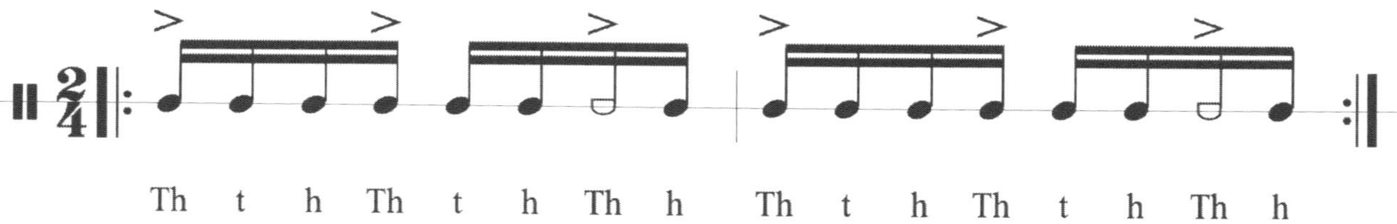

Example 1: Xaxado Variation #1

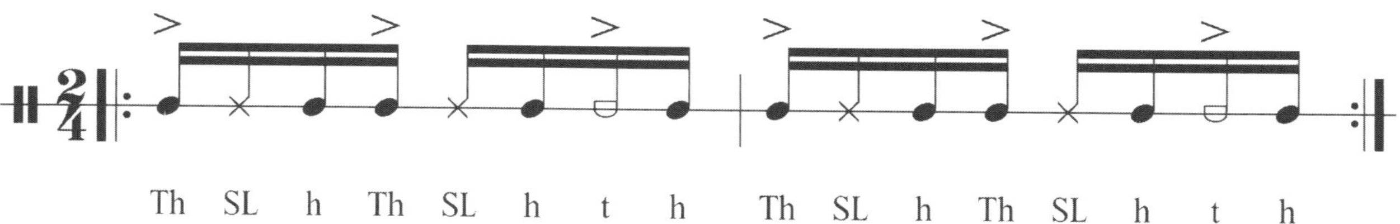

Example 2: Xaxado Variation #2

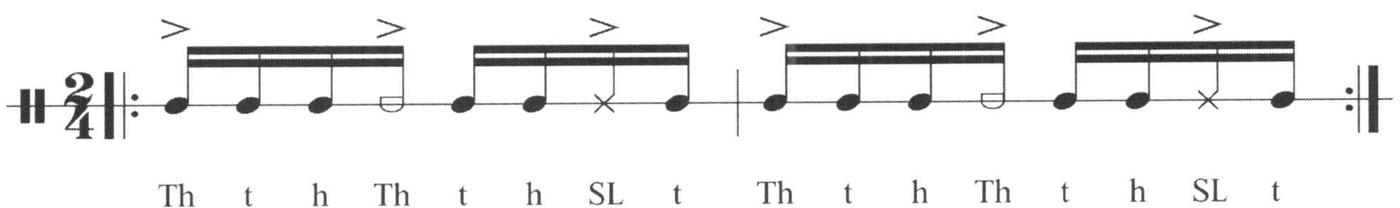

Example 3: Xaxado Variation #3

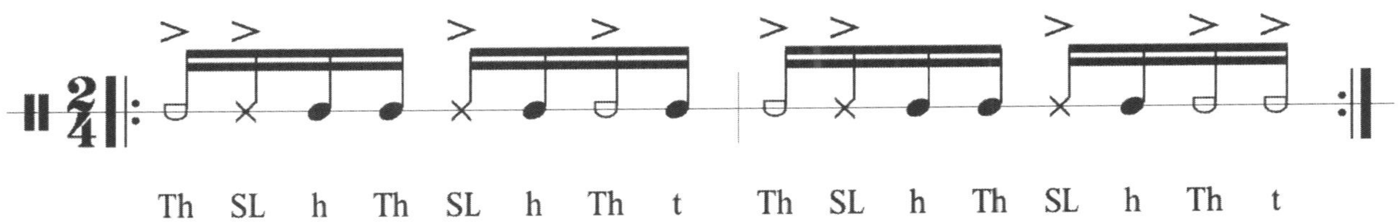

Example 4: Xaxado Variation #4

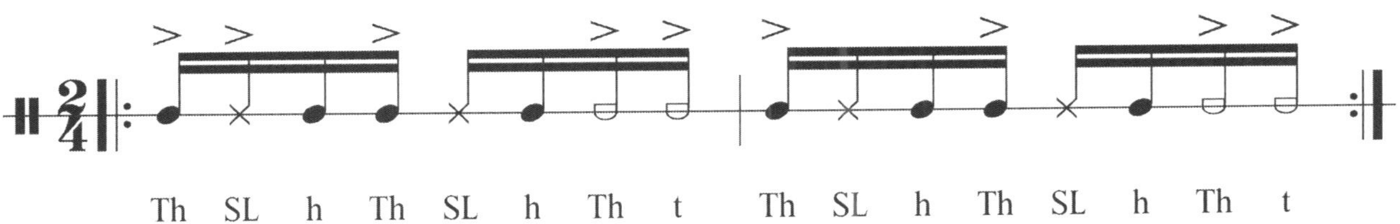

Example 5: Xaxado Variation #5

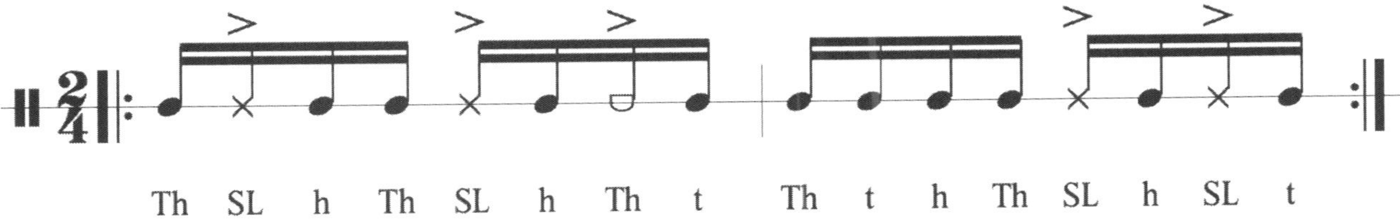

Example 6: Xaxado Variation #6

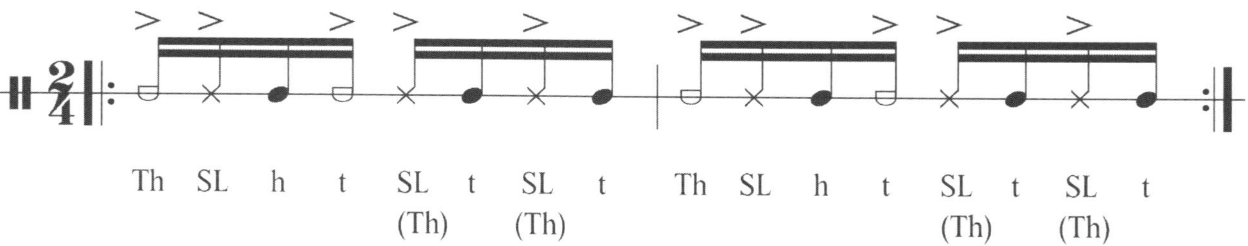

Xaxado Listening Suggestions

- *Xaxado by Luiz Gonzaga*
- *Óia Eu Aqui de Novo by Gilberto Gil*

Chapter 26. Northeastern Brazilian Rhythms: Xote

Xote is usually played at a slower tempo than a baião or côco. Xote evolved in word origin from the European dance, schottische, which is similar to a slow polka and is a partner dance. The schottische was brought to Brazil by the Portuguese and developed further in the Northeast. The emphasis is a heavy swing on the second half of the 2/4 rhythm. Listening to examples is very important to get a sense of the swing.

Xote (Basic rhythm)

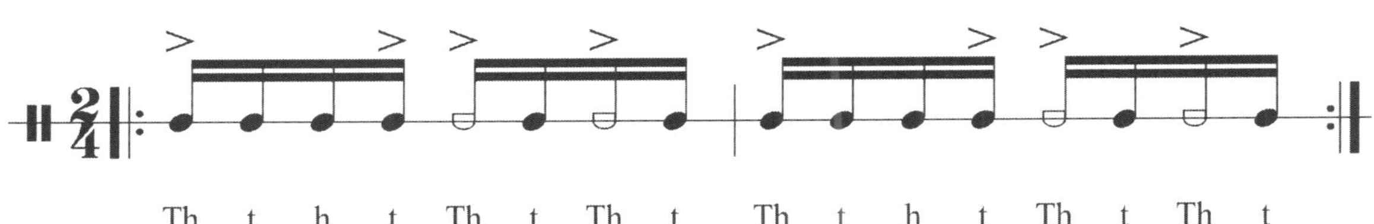

Example 1: Xote Variation #1 adding a slap

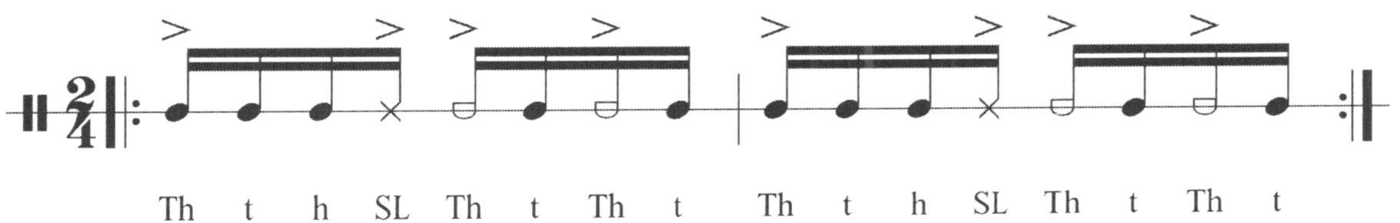

Example 2: Xote Variation #2 combining basic rhythm and example 1

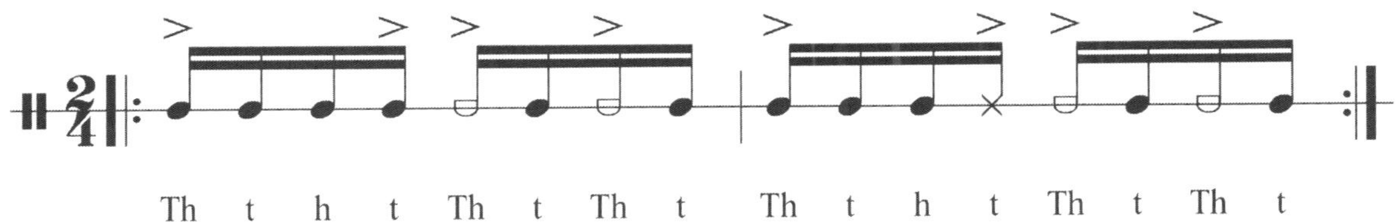

Example 3: Xote Variation #3 with a slightly open tip note on tha "a" of beat 1 just before beat 2

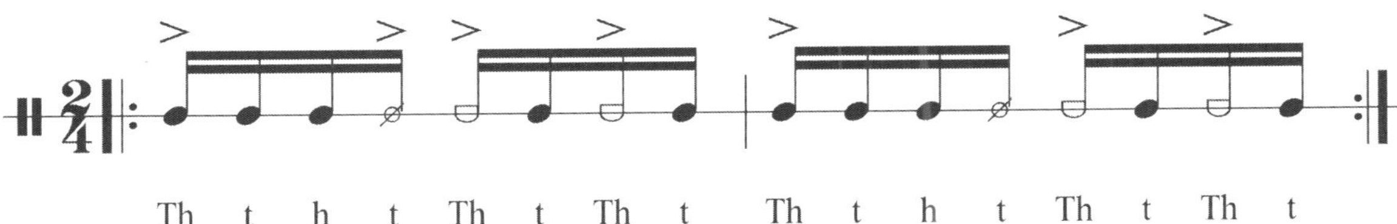

Example 4: Xote Variation #4

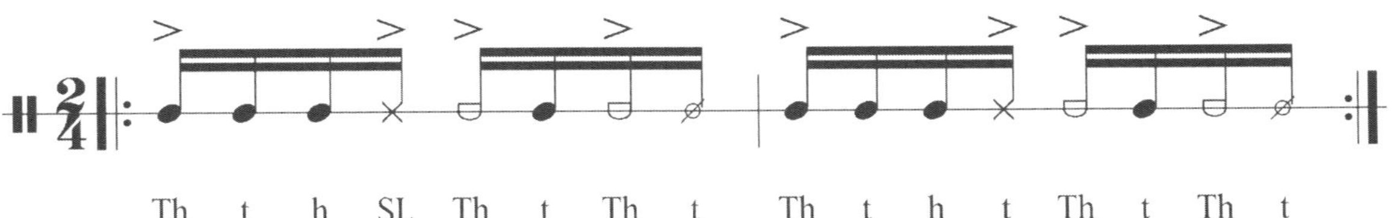

Example 5: Xote Variation #5

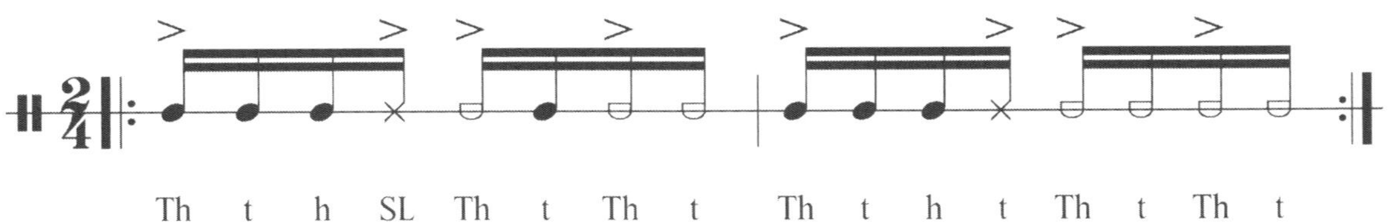

Example 6: Xote Variation #6

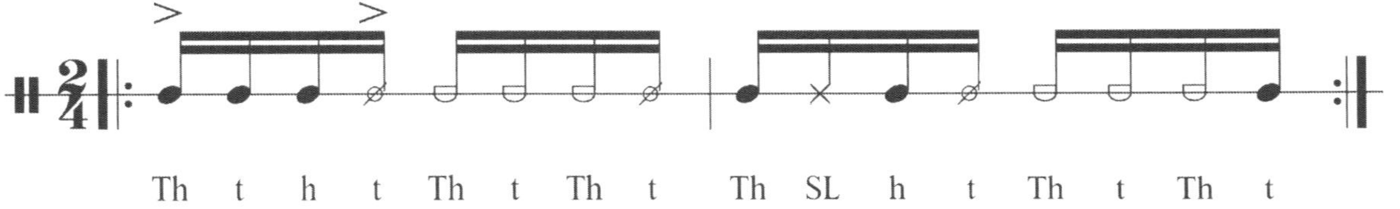

Example 7: Xote Variation #7

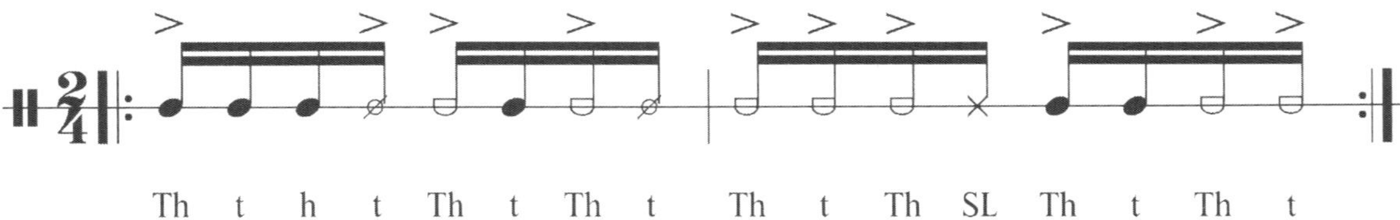

Xote Listening Suggestions

- *Xote das Meninas by Luiz Gonzaga*
- *Sabiá by Luiz Gonzaga*
- *Petrolina Juazeiro by Luiz Gonzaga*

Chapter 27. Ciranda

Ciranda is a dance originally from Recife, Pernambuco from the Ilhã de Itamaracá. Ciranda is danced in a circle, originally by women, with the dance emulating the waves of the ocean. The dance and music use a repetitive rhythm with a relaxed feel and traditional or folkloric instruments. Open notes are played with the surdo in mind and at a slow tempo.

Ciranda

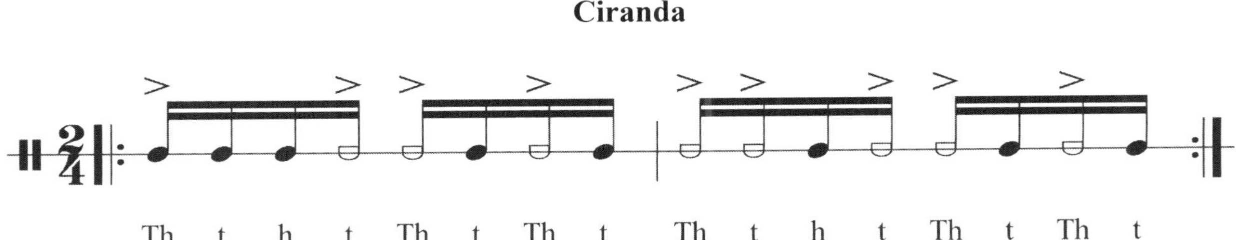

Example 1: Ciranda Variation #1

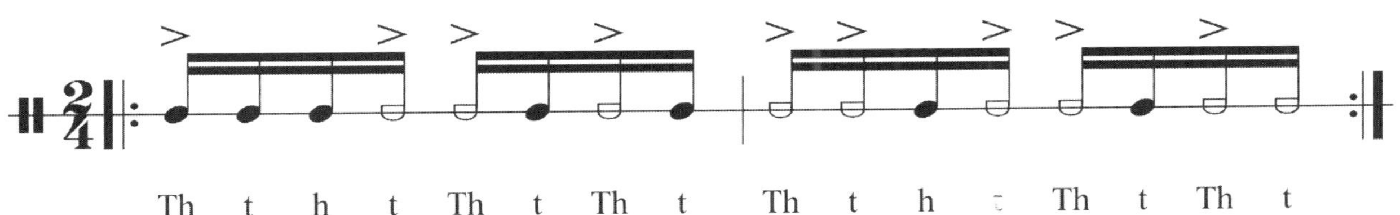

Example 2: Ciranda Variation #2

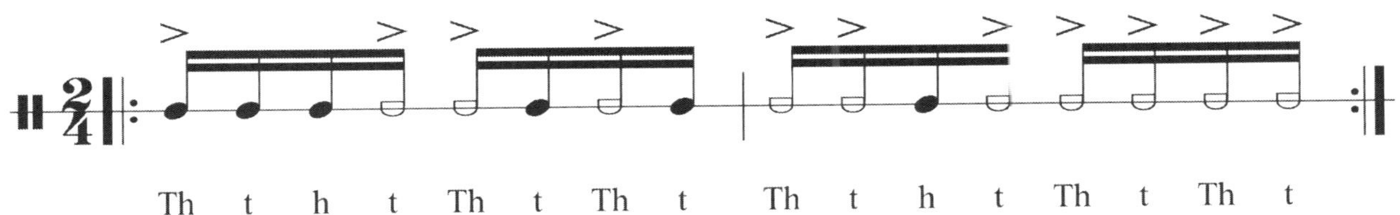

Example 3: Ciranda Variation #3

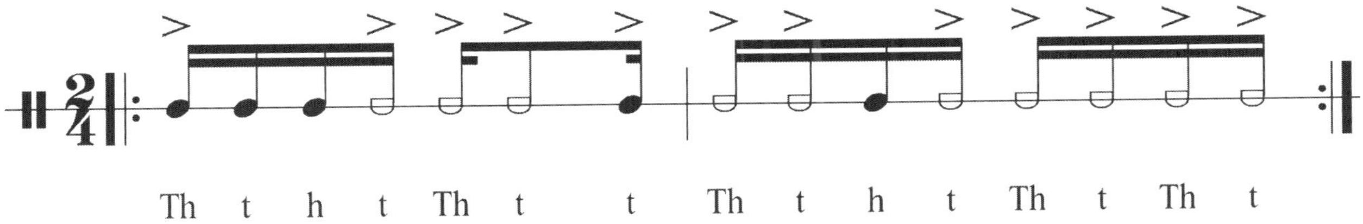

Example 4: Ciranda Variation #4

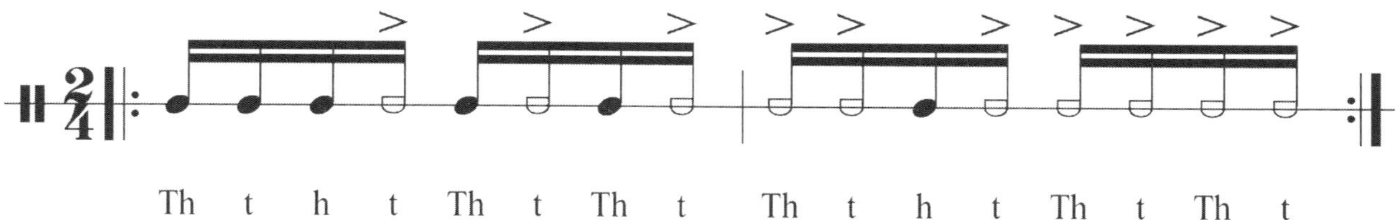

Example 5: Ciranda Variation #5

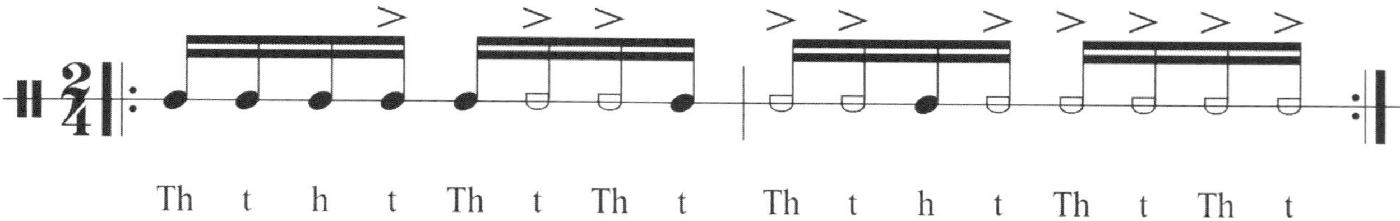

Ciranda Listening Suggestions

- *Eu Sou Lia, Minha Ciranda e Preta Cira by Lia de Itamaracá*
- *Ciranda Cirandinha- child's folk song*
- *Ciranda da Lua -*

Chapter 28. Frevo

Frevo is originally from the Northeast of Brazil in Recife, Pernambuco. Rhythmically it is defined as a gallop, march, or fast polca. Throughout Brazil, several musical styles were derived and developed throughout the 19th century with influence from the brass and marching bands that paraded during Carnaval, festivals and community events as well. There is a great deal to this music and its history and many varying styles of frevo, such as frevo de bloco, and frevo de rua just to name a few styles. For this instruction manual, the following exercises will focus on the fast-paced frevo. Sometimes a frevo sounds more like a march and other times like a polca, and this depends on tempo and the kind of frevo. Tempo can guide on whether to play a march or a frevo. If it's a fast-paced frevo there is no mistaking the rhythms notated below. It's very difficult to play consistently fast and should be practiced. A pandeiro player who can play frevo passes one of the true tests in the mastery of the drum because it requires stamina and endurance. The pattern and fingering may seem simple but are hard to maintain without practice.

The principal pattern that the pandeiro is copying in frevo is the caixa or snare and bass notes emphasize a surdo or large bass drum. This pattern can be played with two tips in a row, thumb-tip-tip or also sometimes thumb-tip-heel.

Example 1

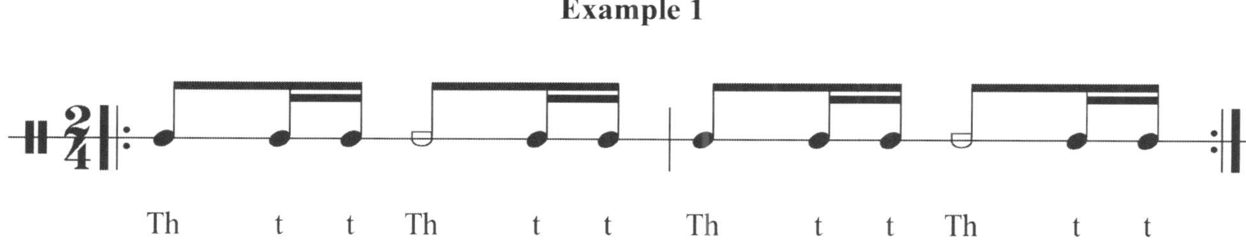

Example 2 with pick-up

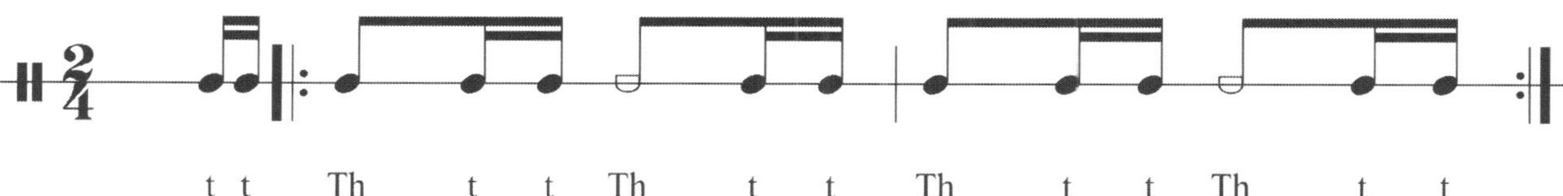

Example 3: Using the same pattern but with a different technique that uses tip-heel.

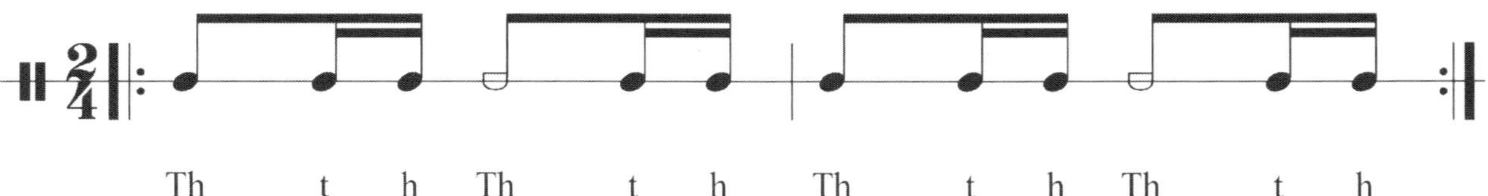

Example 4: Using the same pattern but with a pick-up.

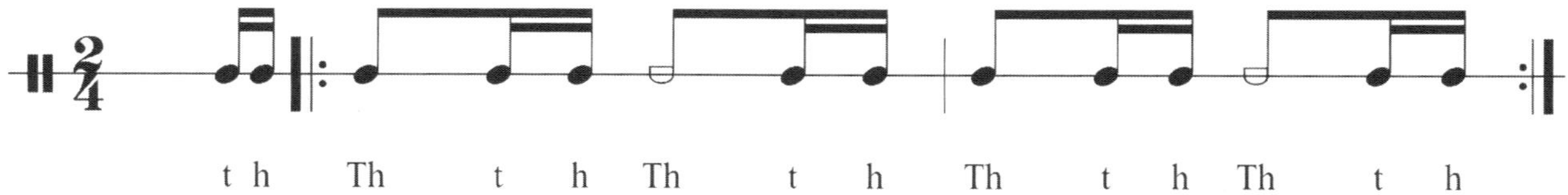

Example 5: Here is a typical turn-around or something that can be played at the end of a phrase or section of music.

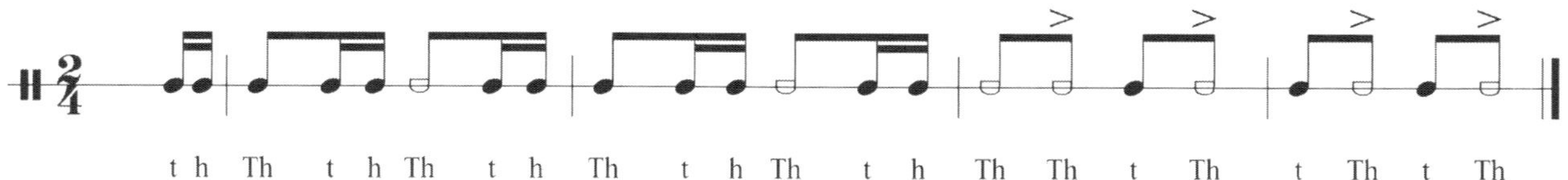

Frevo Listening Suggestions

- *Frevo Pernambuco by Francisco Alves*
- *Ô Abre Alas by Chiquinha Gonzaga*
- *Frevo de Lira by Waldir Azevedo & Luiz Lira*
- *Olha Pra Céu by Luiz Gonzaga & José Fernandes*
- *Ciranda Cirandinha - child's folk song*
- *Taí by Noel Rosa*
- *Taine by Osmar Macêdo*
- *Vassourinhas by Matias da Rocha & Joana Batista*
- *Praça XI by Trio de Ouro (Dalva de Oliveira, Herivelto Martins e Nilo Chagas) e Castro Barbosa*

Chapter 29. Maracatu

Maracatu is a style of music that originates in the northeast of Brazil and is found between the cities of Recife and Olinda in the state of Pernambuco. The music emerged from Africans brought to Brazil through the slave trade from Benin and Central Africa. There are indigenous influences as well. Like many musical styles in Brazil, they emerged from the theme of Carnaval brought to Brazil through the Portuguese with the original Carnevale beginning in Venice, Italy. Many styles will emulate and also distort or satirize the role of the European royal court.

Africans who were enslaved were allowed to congregate and play music during the Carnaval season and as with samba, in maracatu, there is a reference to the king and queen. Maracatu blocos or nations known as "naçãos" involve a coronation of king and queen and a "court" of dukes, barons, ambassadors, etc.

Maracatu has been played since the 17th century and is played with an African-derived bell pattern played on a "gonque," which is the same kind of bell found in many West and Central African drum cultures. In addition, the main instruments include snare drum parts or "caixa" parts, shekeres and shakers or "ganzás," as well as a bass drum made of wood and skin drams called "alfaias." Alfaias are tuned by pulling the heavy cord that holds the drumhead on the drum.

"Baques" are rhythms that distinguish between the varying blocos or naçãos. For the purpose of this book, this is an introduction to one style of maracatu and patterns adapted for pandeiro, a pattern that is common but not always the most traditional maracatu bell. There are many styles of maracatu and this is but one example.

As mentioned above, there are several bell patterns that match different rhythms in maracatu. The bell is often played on what is called a "gonque" bell and is a descendent of the African bell.

Bell pattern of the Maracatu: "Baque de Arrasto"

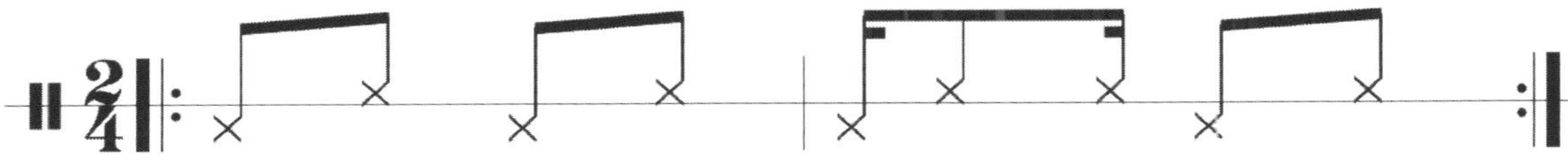

Bell Pattern of the Maracatu: "Baque de Arrasto" adapted/ played on pandeiro starting on the thumbs

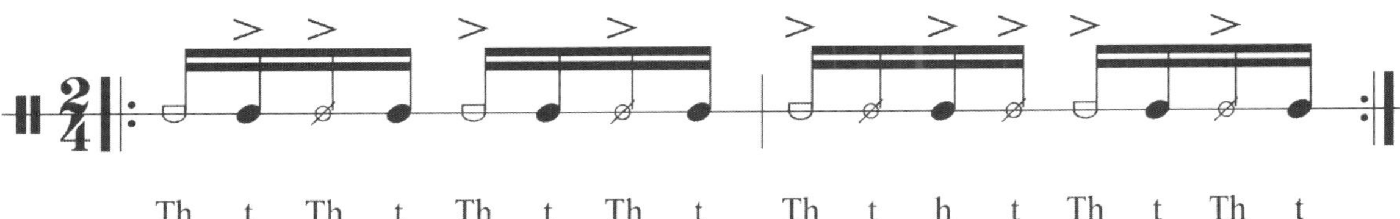

The following examples are adaptations of the Alfaias for Pandeiro:

Example 1: Baque de Arrasto Alfaia pattern adapted for pandeiro starting on the thumb

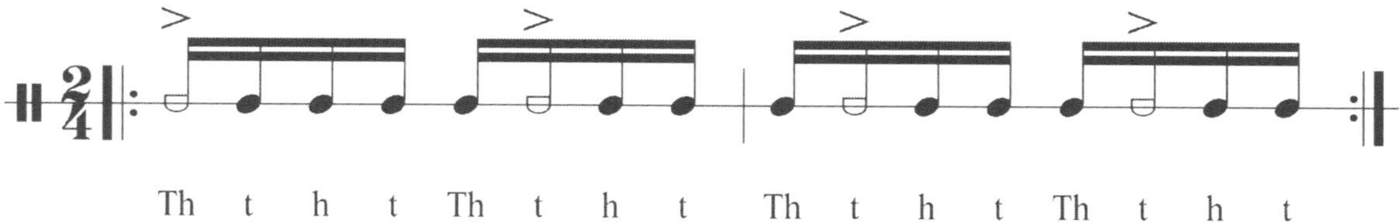

Example 1a: Example 1: Baque de Arrasto Alfaia pattern adapted for pandeiro starting on tips

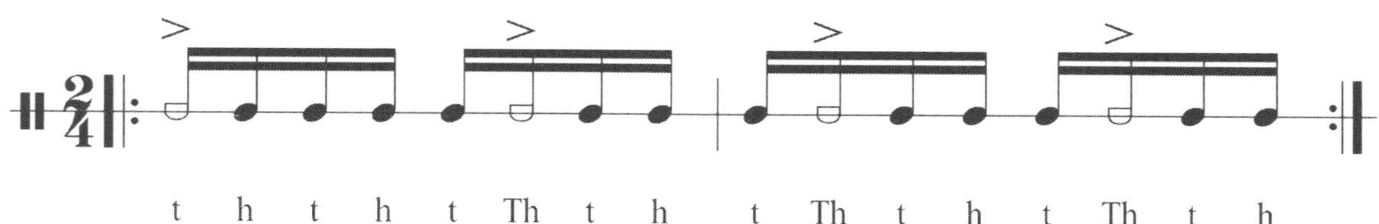

Example 2: Maracatu variation starting on the tips

Example 3: Maracatu variation starting on the tips

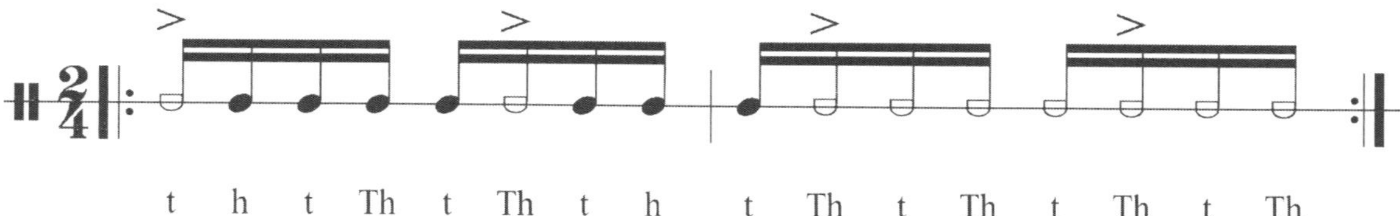

Example 4: A fusion/hybrid of maracatu and funk pattern: *Maraca-Funk*

Example 5: A fusion/hybrid of maracatu and funk pattern: *Maraca-Funk*

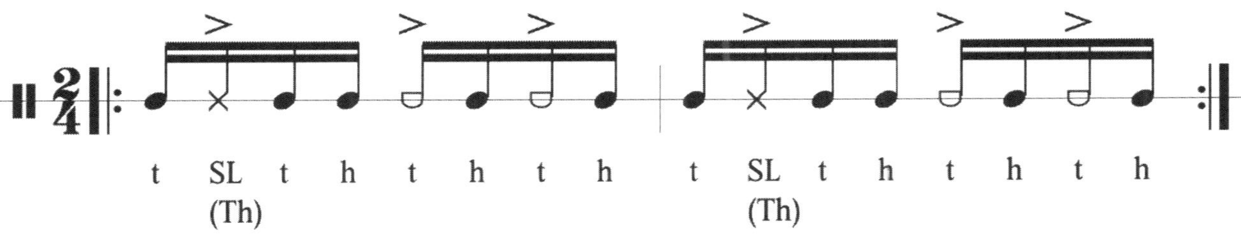

Maracatu Listening Suggestions

- *Baque-Forte (album) by Maracatu Nação Encanto da Alegria*
- *Nossos Tambores Maracatu Nação Estrela Brilhante do Recife by Grupo Yalu*
- *Cheguei Meu Povo by Maracatu Estrela Brilhante do Recife*
- *Estrela Brilhante de Igarassu 180 Anos by Grupo Estrela Brilhante*

Chapter 30. Partido Alto

Partido alto is a variation of the samba pattern. It translates to "high part" because if there are two pandeiro players in samba, one percussionist might play the partido alto and the other percussionist the main samba groove. It's both a style of music as well as a pattern and is used heavily in pagode, samba and is referenced in samba and even choro. Baden Powell used this rhythm heavily in his afro-sambas and songs like "Canto de Ossanha, Berimbau, and Consolação" where songs move between partido alto and samba patterns. There are other names for the syncopated rhythms like partido alto such as batuque, afro-samba, samba-afro, pagode, etc.

Basic Partido Alto

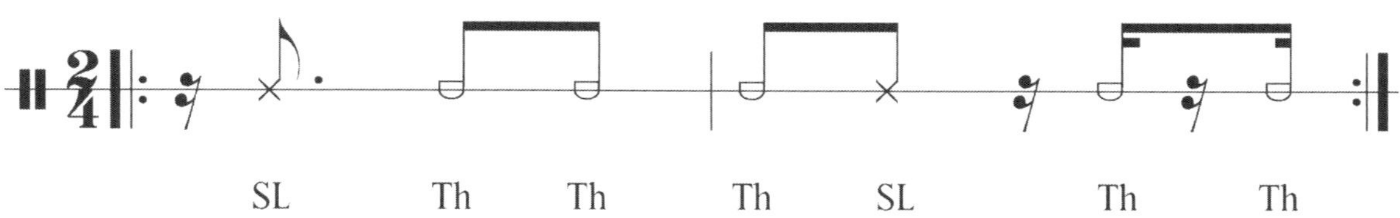

Example 1: Partido Alto Variation #1

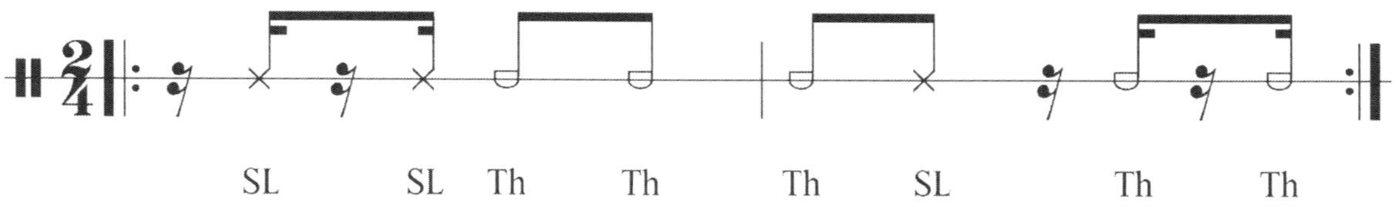

Example 2: Partido Alto Variation #2

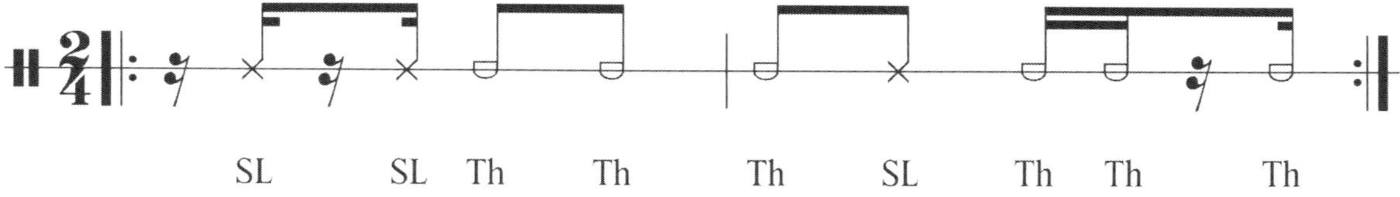

Example 3: Partido Alto Variation #3

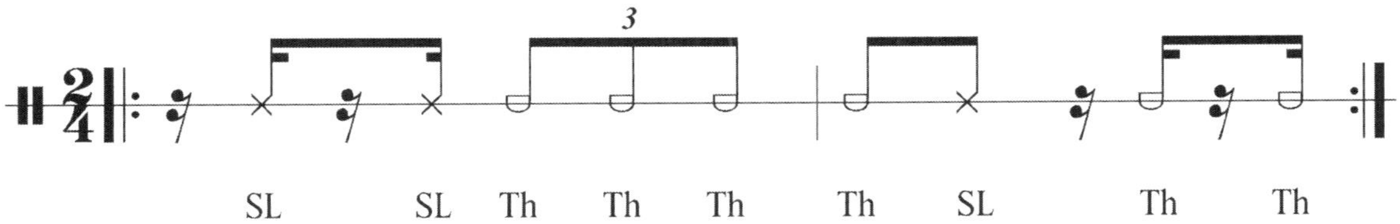

Example 4: Partido Alto Variation #4

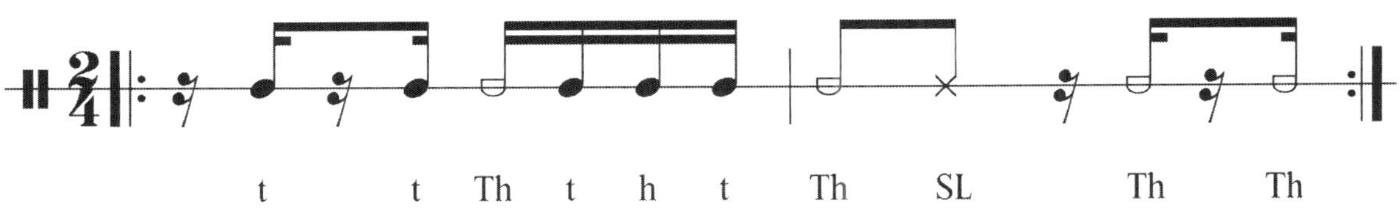

Example 5: Partido Alto Variation #5

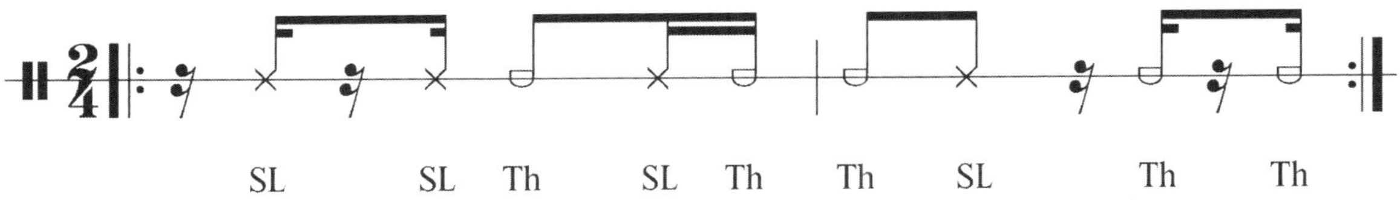

Example 6: Partido Alto Variation #6

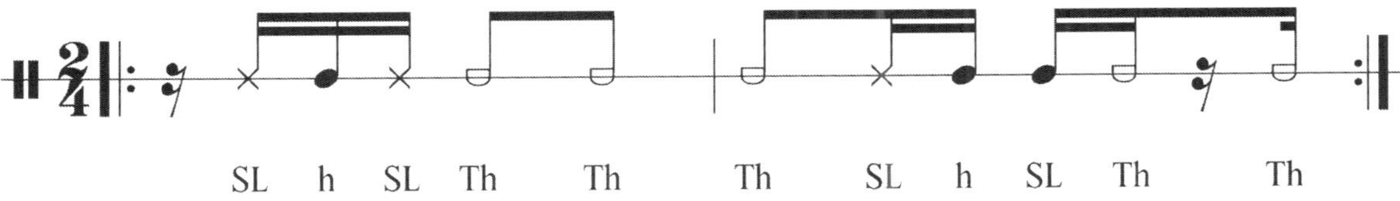

Example 7: Partido Alto Variation #7

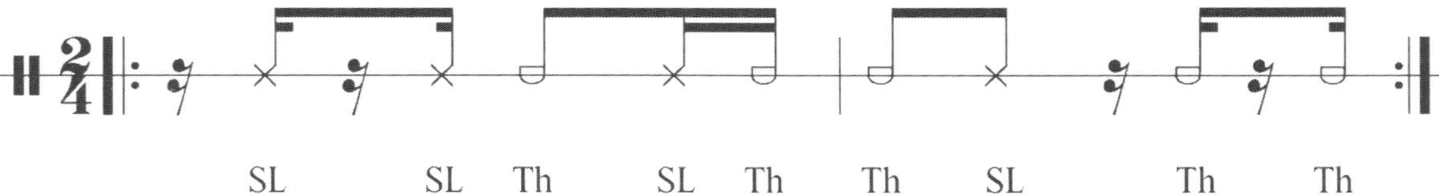

Listening Suggestions

- *Partido Alto, short documentary film (1982) directed by Leon Hirszman and produced by Emrafilme.*
- *De Qualquer Maneira by Candeia*
- *Lucidez by Jorge Aragåo*
- *Vai lá, Vai lá by Fundo do Quintal*
- *Quando a Gira Girou by Zeca Pagodeiro*

Chapter 31. Afro-Samba Rhythms

Afro-Samba rhythms have many variations and styles and can be a specific rhythm or more generic for an Afro-Samba inspired rhythm to which there are many, many variations. For example, samba de roda which is a samba danced in a circle, is one of the oldest forms of samba dance and music. Samba de roda became popular and blossomed out of its popularity in Rio de Janeiro via "Baianos" (people from the state of Bahia in the northeast) who migrated to Rio de Janeiro in the late 19th century of Afro-Brazilian origin.

Pagode, samba da mesa, samba-funk, samba do pê, and samba de breque are just a few examples of the myriad styles of samba. Pagode is often played around a table with a heavy percussion section, cavaquinho, and songs. It is another style of music that uses partido alto and came onto the music scene in Rio de Janeiro in the 1970s and became very popular in the 1980s through a musical group, "Fundo de Quintal." Originally, pagode meant a party or gathering with food and music. Many samba-school instruments were used with the hardware stripped down to play as hand percussion instruments that were more portable, (vs. stick-hand or sticks and in parade format) which resulted in a whole new line of Brazilian percussion instruments being formed. Songs will rhythmically contain patterns or rhythms with names such as: partido alto, samba, batuque, afro, samba-afro, and afro-samba. Below are a few examples of Afro-Samba.

Afro-Samba - Basic Pattern for Pandeiro

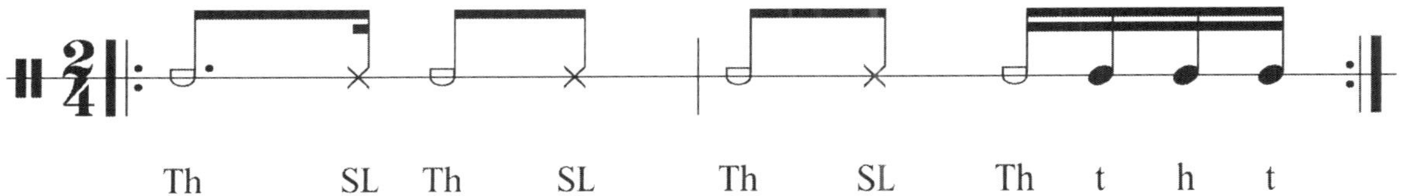

Example 1: Afro-Samba Variation #1

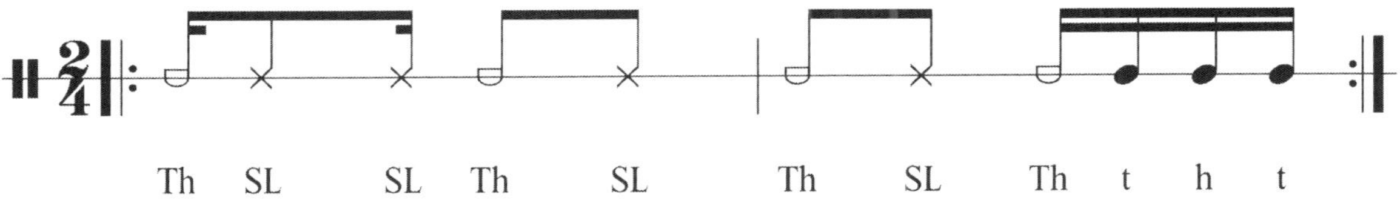

Example 2: Afro-Samba Variation #2

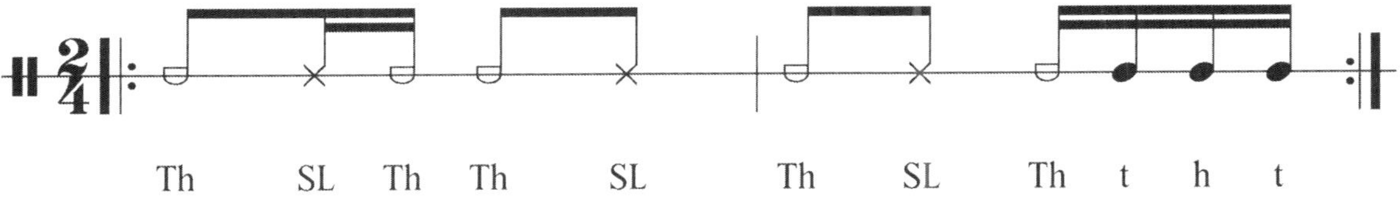

Example 3: Afro-Samba Variation #3

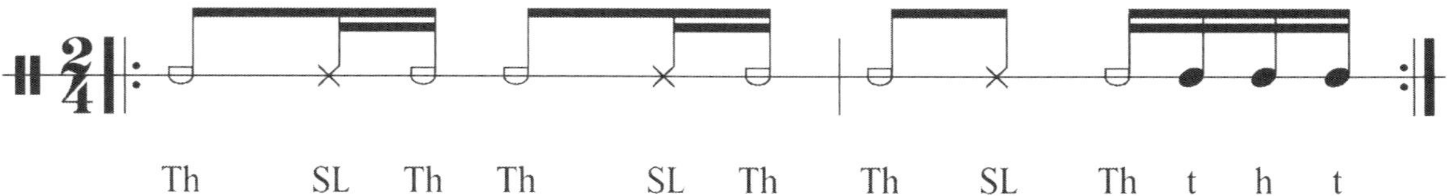

Example 4: Afro-Samba Variation #4

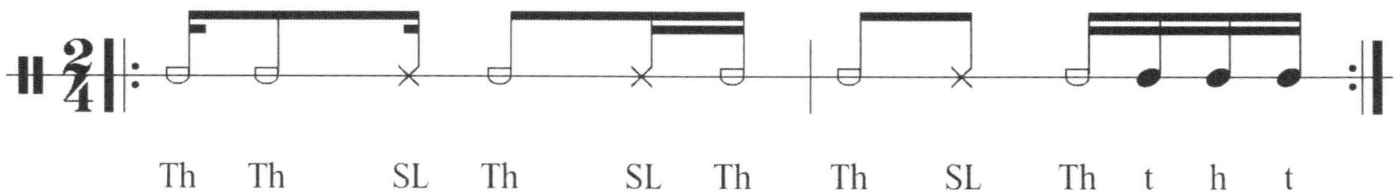

Example 5: Afro-Samba Variation #5

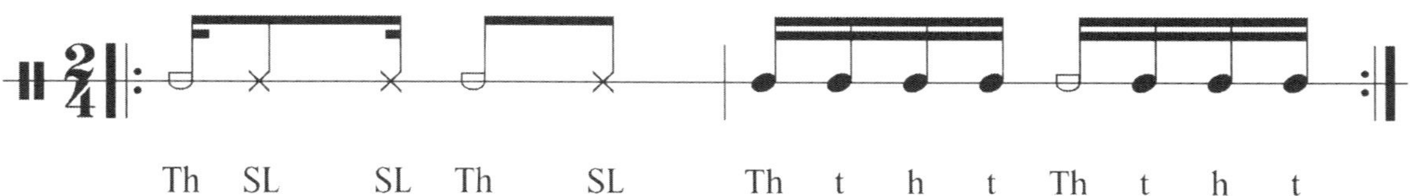

Example 6: Afro-Samba Variation #6

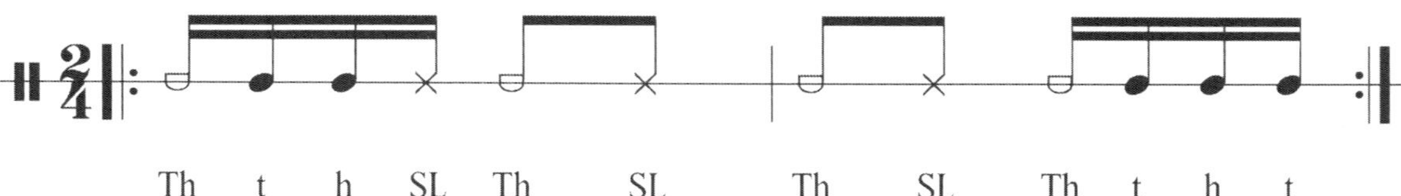

Chapter 32. A Valsa

A valsa or "waltz" is one of the musical styles encapsulated under the style of "choro." The valsa became popular in Brazil during the mid to early 19th century. Globally, the waltz has made its way into almost every culture, tradition and music in the Western world. It's in 3/4 time and traditionally played at a slower tempo. It is found as a European classical dance and folk-dance tradition. Of course, traditionally there is no pandeiro in the valsa.

The Brazilian waltz was popular and incorporated different musical genres from classical music, popular music, and folkloric/African music. There are several kinds of waltz genres such as the valsa Espanola (Spanish waltz) or valsa Sertenejo.

The Brazilian waltz is the same groove as a traditional waltz. However, there are double-time waltzes that are felt in a 6/8 feel. These examples below show how the pandeiro can accompany this double-time waltz with a more 6/8 feel.

Written 6/8 or called Valsa Dobrada

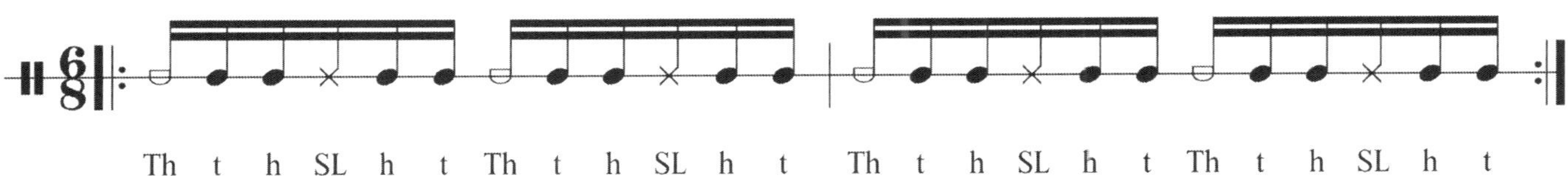

Examples of Valsa Dobrada

A good example of the "valsa dobrada" is in the choro-valsa, "Santa Morena" by Jacob do Bandolim. Another example, by the same composer, is "O Voô da Mosca" which translated means "Flight of the Fly" and is inspired by "Flight of the Bumble-Bee" by Nikolai Rimsky-Korsakov for his opera "The Teale of Tsar Saltan" which was composed in 1899-1900.

An example of a valsa dobrada groove for "Santa Morena" by Jacob do Bandolim

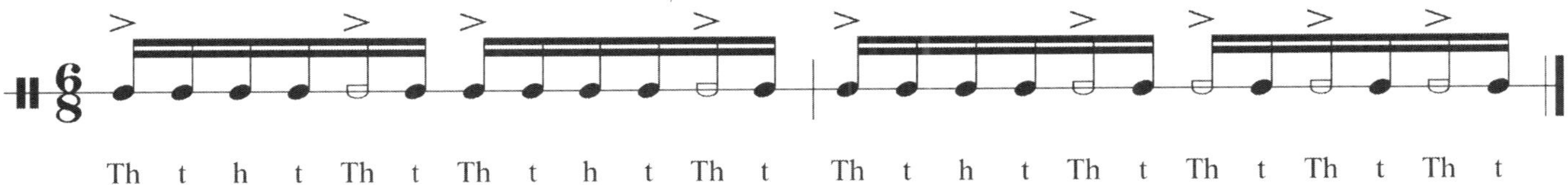

Example 1: Slight change with Accents

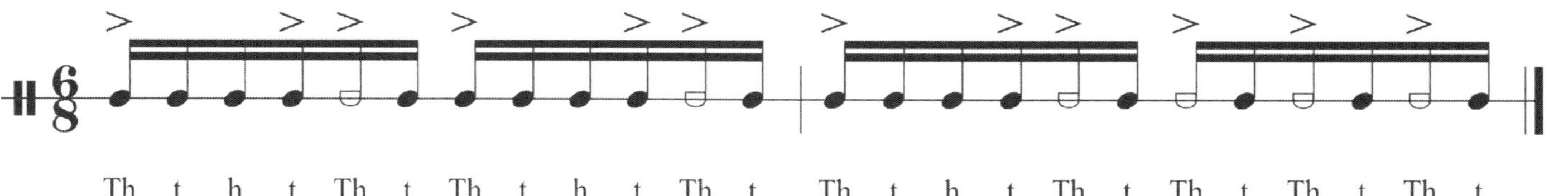

Example 2

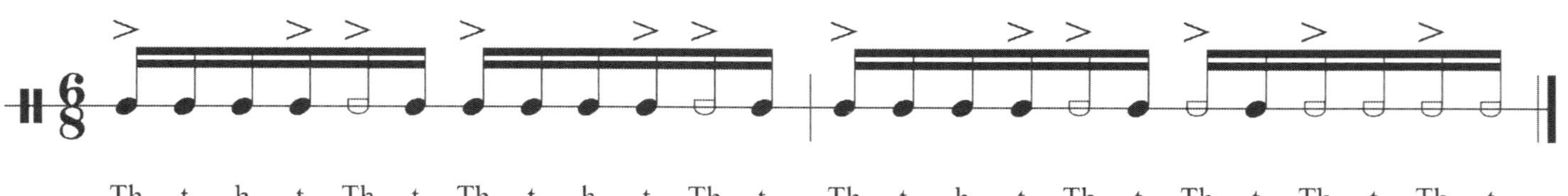

Example 3

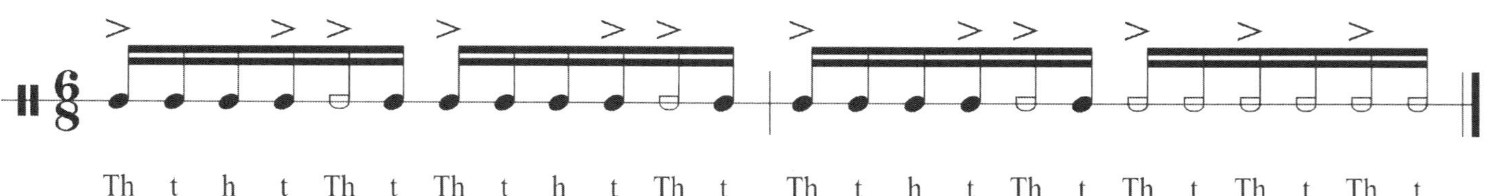

Example for "O Voô da Mosca" by Jacob do Bandolim

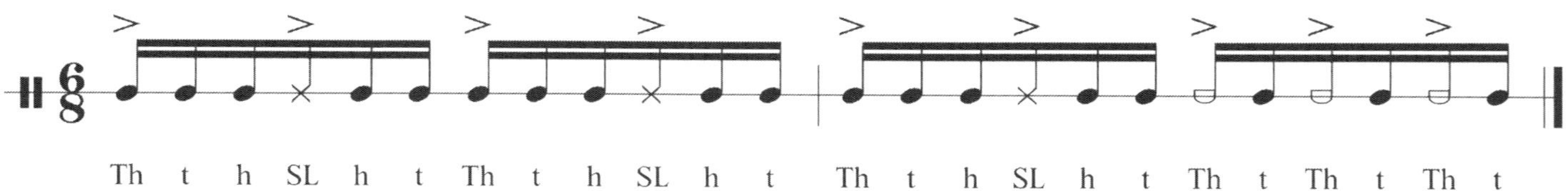

Example 1

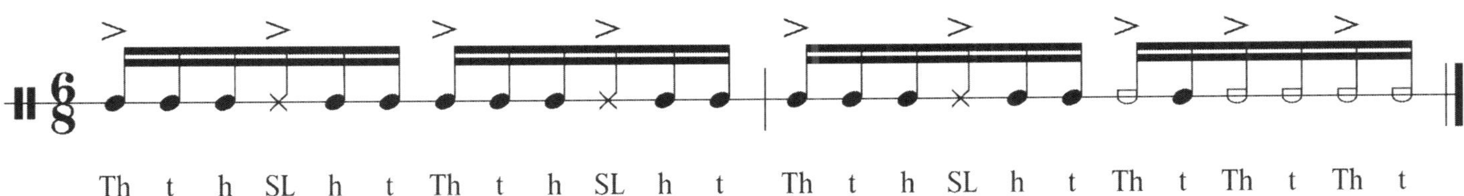

Example 2

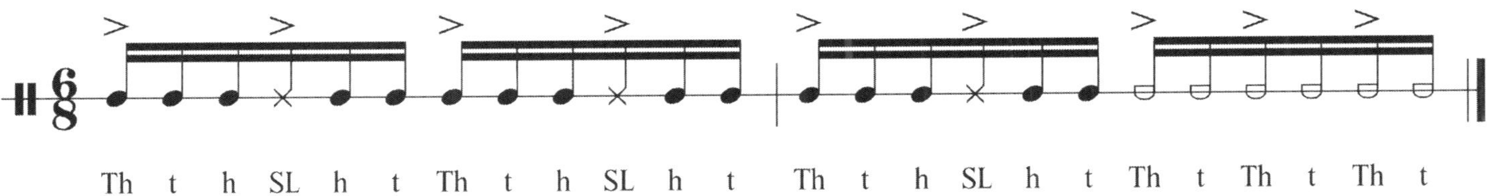

Listening Suggestions

- *Santa Morena by Jacob do Bandolim*
- *O Voô da Mosca by Jacob do Bandolim*
- *Chamamé by Yamandu Costa*

Chapter 33. Samba in 3

Samba in 3 is not commonplace in samba as it is an odd meter. Emphasis can be placed in 3/4 or 6/8-time signature while still emphasizing a 2/4 samba but in 3/4 time. The first rhythm notated below is from the song, "Cravo e Canela" which means "Clove and Cinnamon" and is a samba in 3 recorded by Milton Nascimento and Lô Borges in 1972. Milton Nascimento was born in Rio de Janeiro but was raised in Minas Gerais where Congada and several styles of music are in 3/4 and 6/8-time signatures. This is not the only samba in 3 but it's good to know about.

Samba Groove in 3 for "Cravo e Canela"

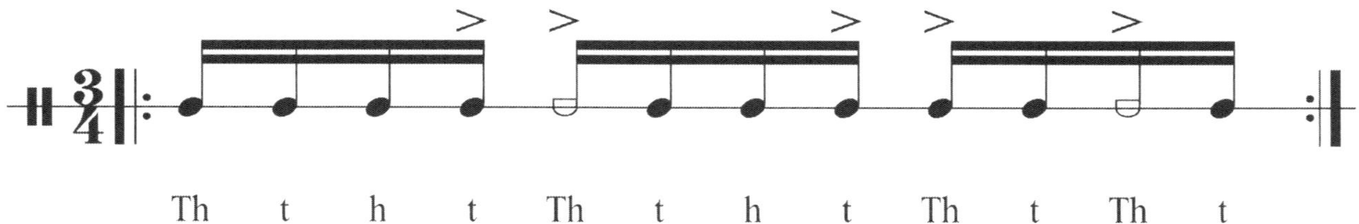

Example 1: Samba in 3 variation

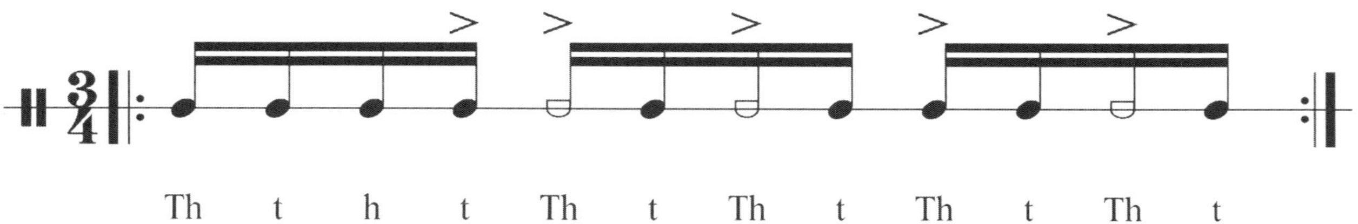

Example 2: Samba in 3 variation

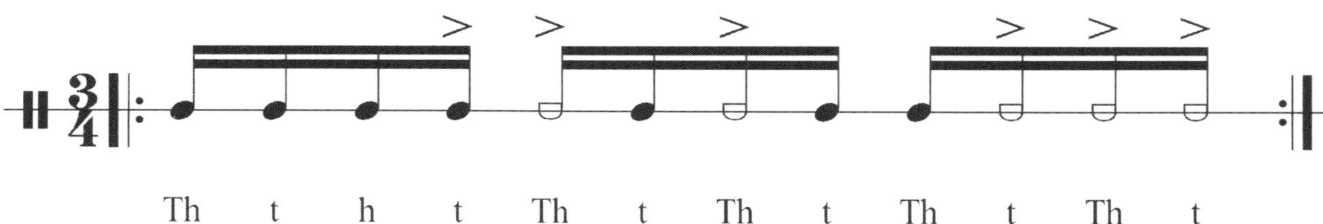

Example 3: Samba in 3 variation by adding a slap before beat 2 but emphasizing open notes on beat 3

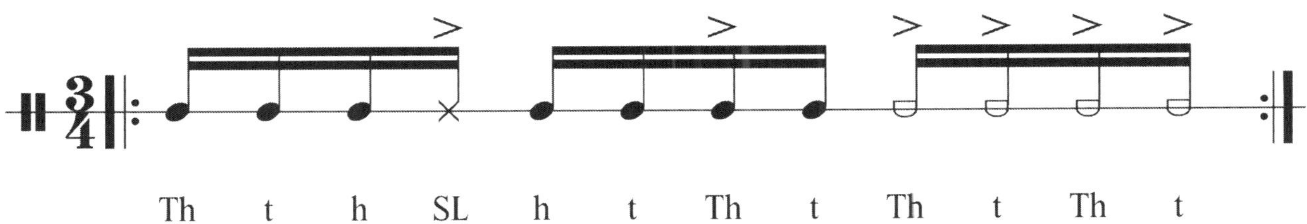

Example 4: Samba in 3 variation

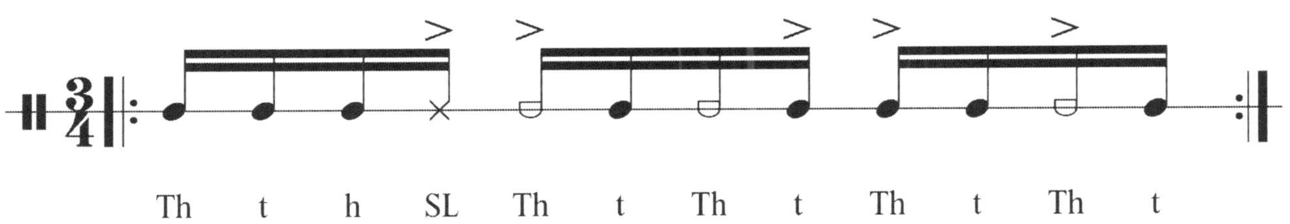

Example 5: Samba in 3 variation

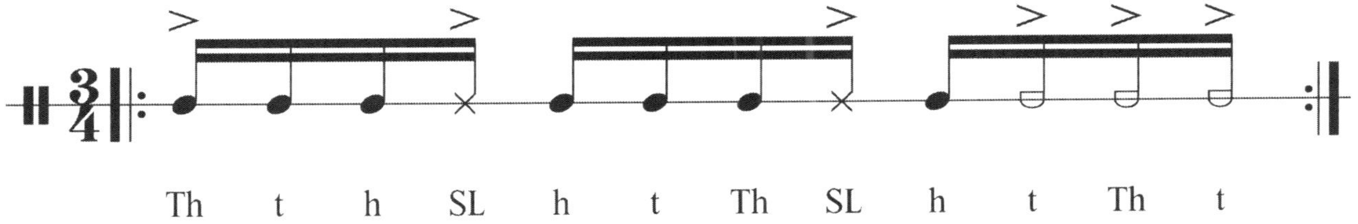

Example 6: Samba in 3 variation with emphasis on beat 2 open notes

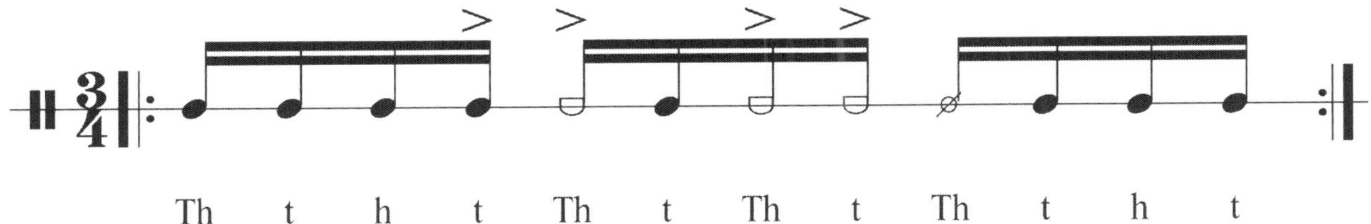

Example 7: Samba in 3 variation

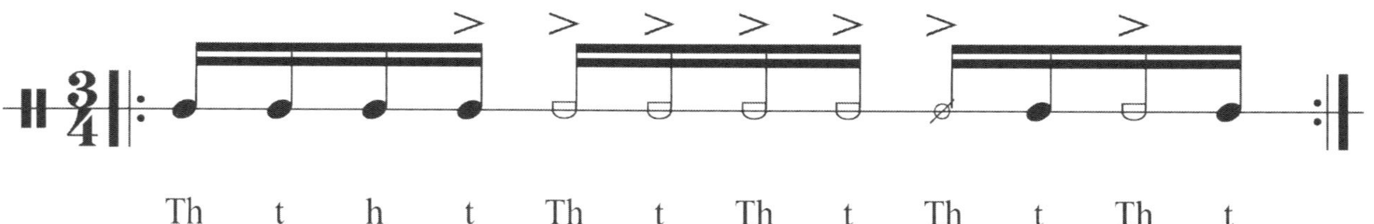

Example 8: Samba in 3 variation

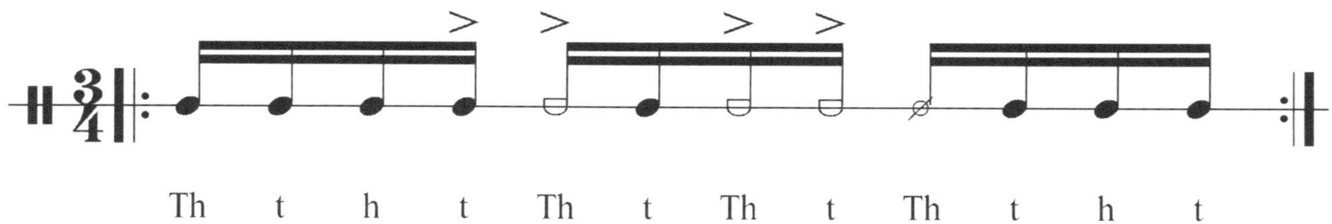

Example 9: Samba in 3 variation

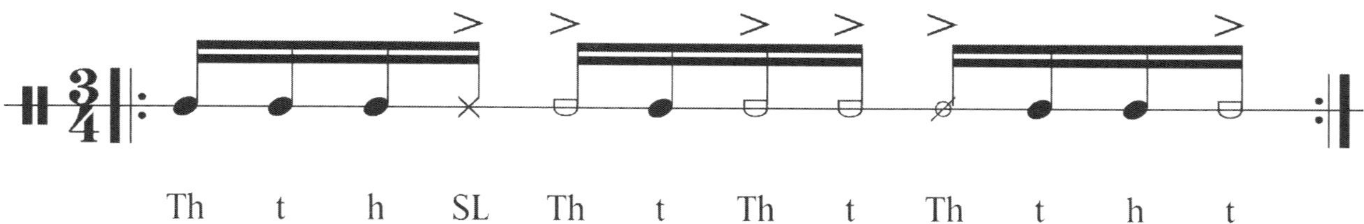

Samba in 3 or 6 Listening Suggestions

- *Cravo e Canela by Milton Nascimento*
- *Paraty by Nilson Matta*
- *Festa de Erê by Jovino Santos Neto*
- *Romance of Death by Airto Moriera*

Chapter 34. Samba in 7

A samba pattern in 7 makes sense for Brazilian music if you divide the 7/8 time to favor accenting a grouping of 4 and then 3. The first half of the pattern can be played just like a 2/4 samba, with the second half in three. The swing and feel will be dominated by the first half of the pattern by just omitting the last two 16th notes of a 4/4 pattern as seen in the examples below. While this is not a typical attribute of samba, there are examples in more contemporary music

Samba in 7

Example 1: Samba in 7 with accents

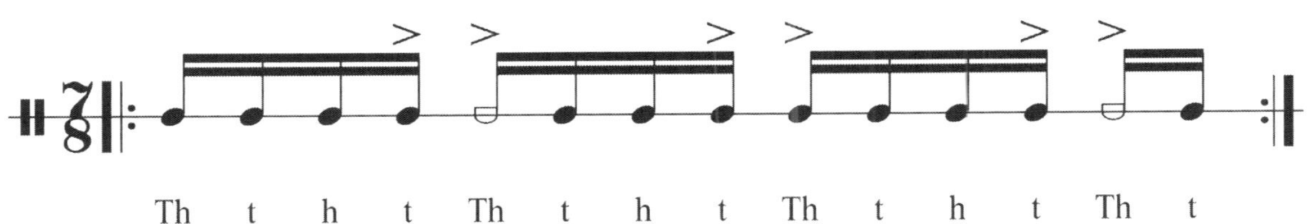

Example 2: Samba variation in 7 with accents and two open tones

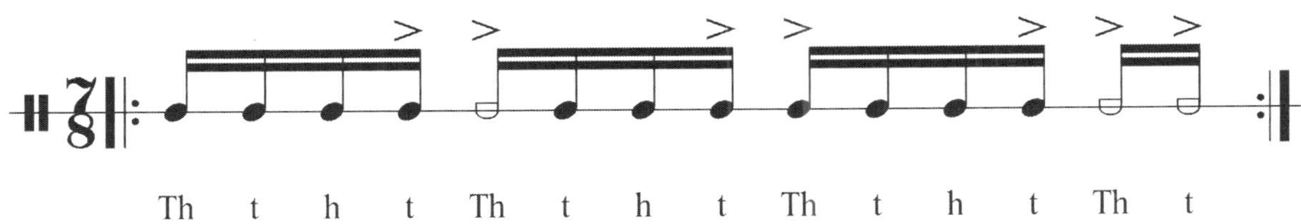

Example 3: Samba variation in 7 with added slap

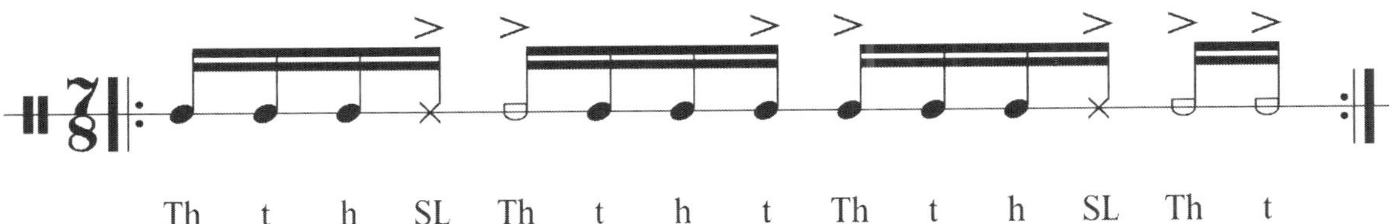

Example 4: Samba variation in 7 with added open tones

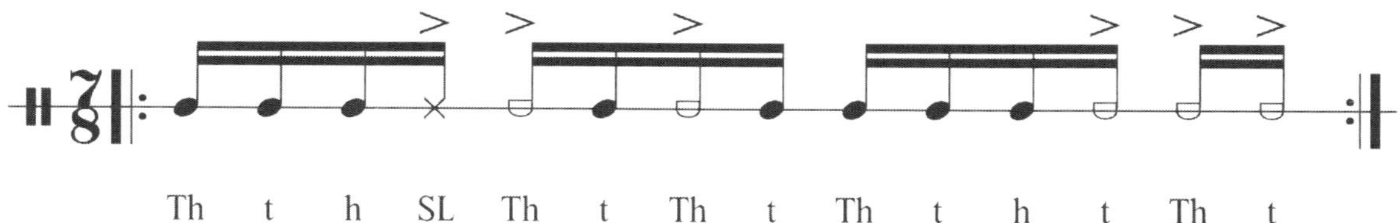

Example 5: Samba variation in 7 with upbeat accents

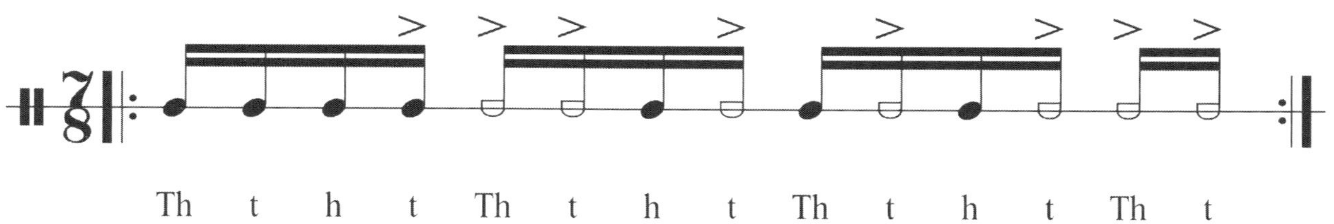

Example 6: Samba variation

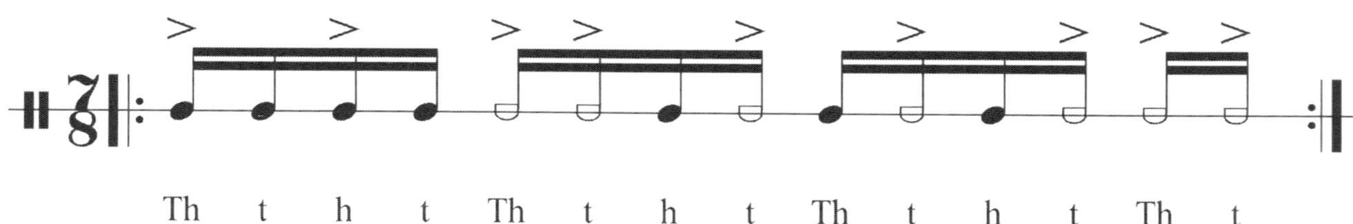

Example 7: Playing around with the tamborim levada (ride) in 7. The first part of the rhythm is like the tamborim pattern in chapter 18.

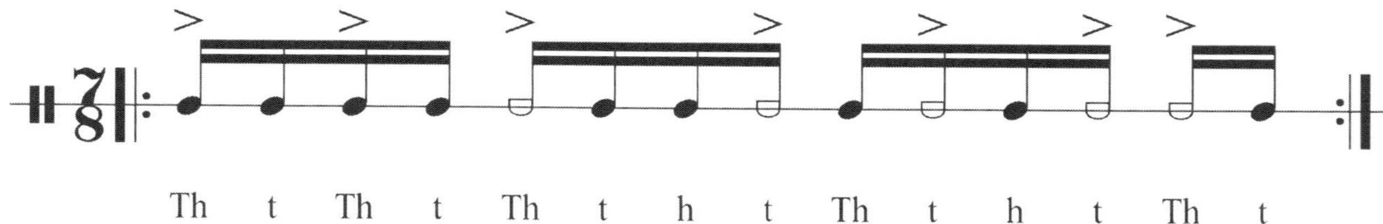

Example 8

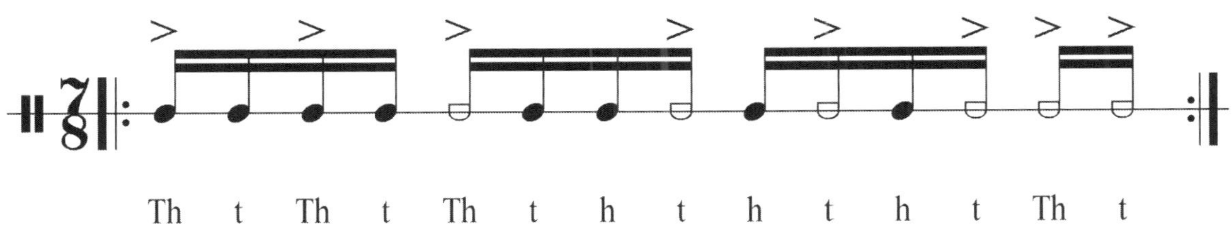

Example 9

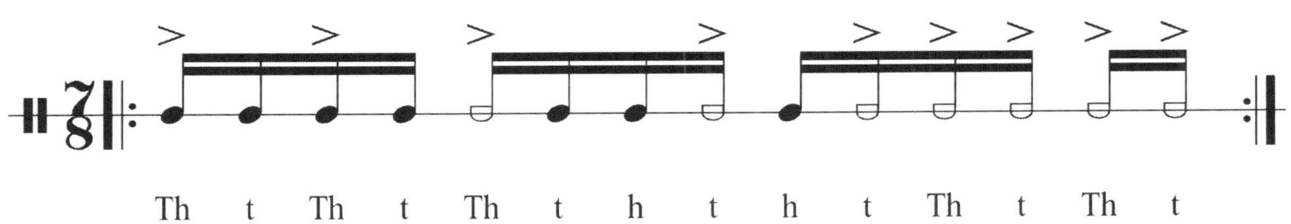

Example 10

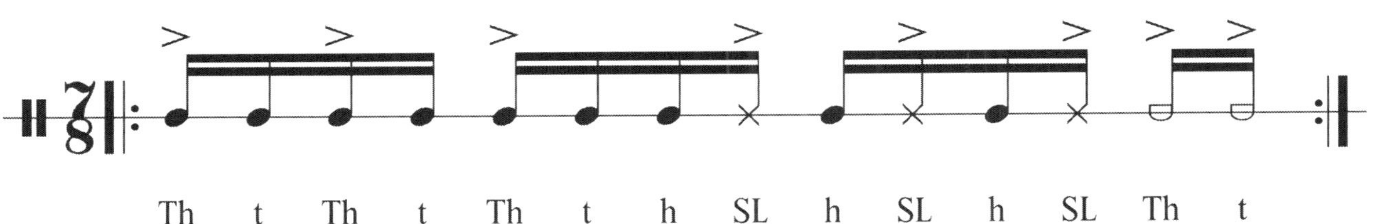

Samba in 7 Listening Suggestions

- *Tacho by Hermeto Pascoal*
- *Música Das Nuvens e Do Chão by Hermeto Pascoal*
- *Tombo in 7/4 by Airto Moreira*
- *Mixing by Airto Moreira*
- *Sempre Sim by Jovino Santos Neto*

Chapter 35. Atabaque or Afoxé Patterns

Candomblé is an Afro-Brazilian religion that began in Brazil with the Atlantic slave trade of the 16th and 17th centuries and continues to develop throughout Brazil. Candomblé is widely influenced directly by Yoruba, Fon, and Bantu African religions and is known as the nation of Candomblé. It is a nature-based religion that celebrates the Orixás (gods of nature) with music (drumming) and dance.

Each nation has its own musical rhythms that are known to them as well as songs, prayers, dances, and specific Orixás. In the Candomblé tradition, the music consists of three drums with the Rum being the lowest, the Rumpi being the middle drum and Lé being the highest-pitched drum. Ijexá and afoxé rhythms are derived directly from Candomblé and have become more secular but many additional musical references to Candomblé culturally, historically, and musically and can be referenced in all aspects of Brazilian culture and should be studied on their own. Below are three basic parts for the three drums adapted for pandeiro.

Rumpi

Example 1: Rumpi Variation #1

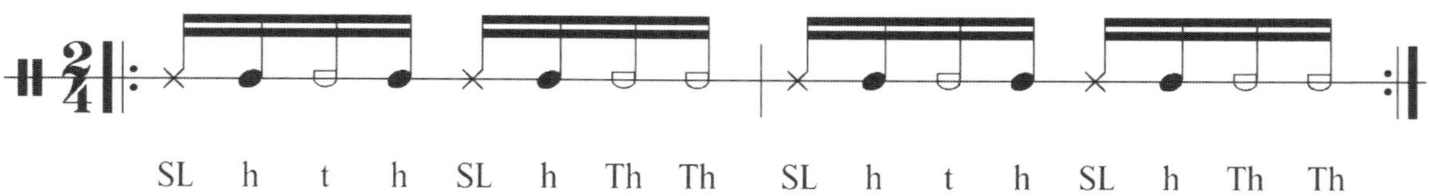

Rum

Chapter 36. Afoxé Patterns

Afoxé styles of music are also sometimes called "Ijexá" which is also a sect of Candomblé. Many African rhythms with origins from the Afro-Brazilian Yoruba-based religion, Candomblé, have become secular. Another name for afoxé is "street Candomblé or Candomblé de rua.

This rhythm below of Ijexá is used in several non-religious musical styles in Bahia and Pernambuco. One famous example is a group called "Os Filhos de Gandhi" or Sons of Gandhi. Ijexá became known widely and is used as a secular musical style with roots in Candomblé and can be found in MPB, axé, samba reggae, Brazilian jazz, or contemporary Brazilian styles of music.

A Traditional Bell Pattern for Ijexá/ Afoxé

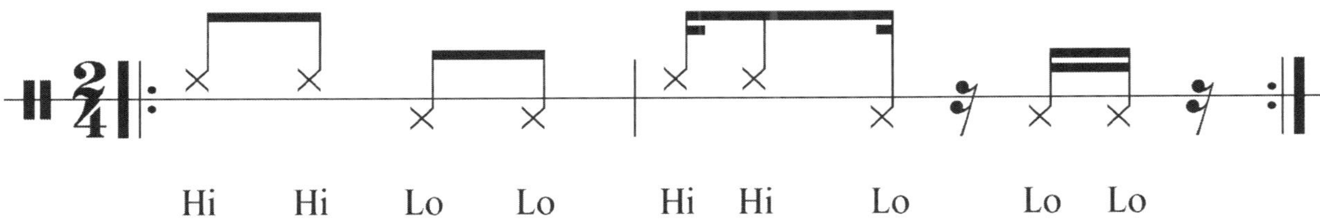

The Bell Pattern adapted for Pandeiro

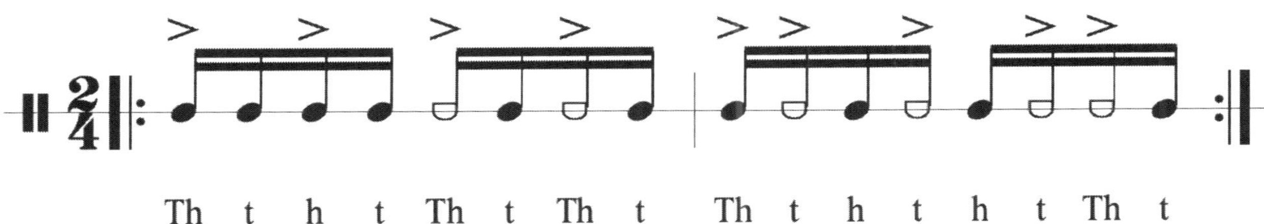

Basic Afoxé Pattern adapted from a conga or Brazilian atabaque drum

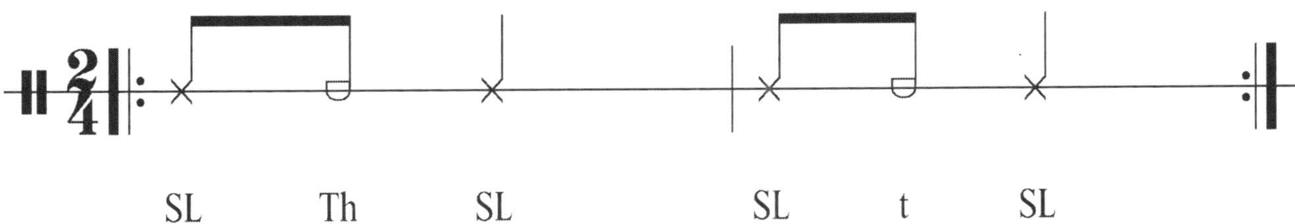

Basic Afoxé Pattern adapted with constant 16th notes forPandeiro

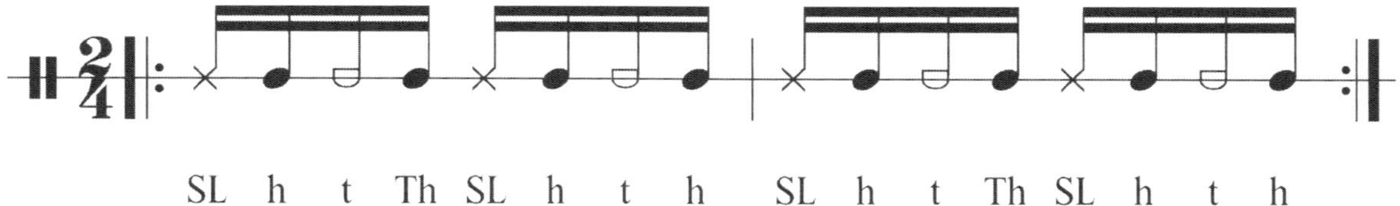

Example 1: Afoxé Variation

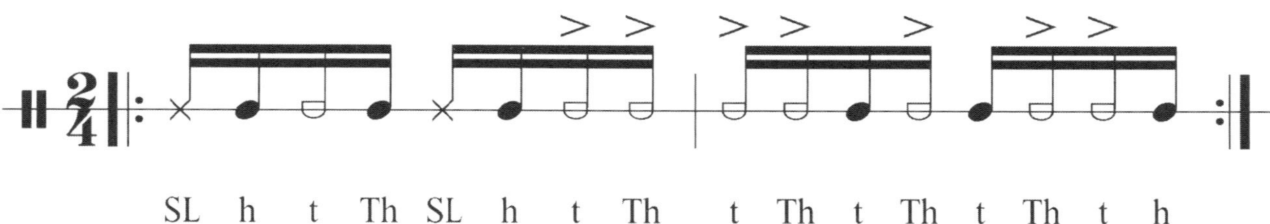

Listening Suggestions

- *Ijexá by Clara Nunes*
- *Filhos de Gandhi by Gilberto Gil*
- *Akará by Margareth Menezes*

Chapter 37. Funk Patterns

Funk and R&B musical styles have migrated the world over. In the 1960s, MPB Música Popular Brasileira (Brazilian Popular Music) or Brazilian pop music was fusing Brazilian samba, northeastern musical styles with rock and jazz influences. Artists like Jorge Ben Jor, Ivan Lins, Gal Costa, and Gilberto Gil were big pioneers of this sound.

In 1993 the singer-songwriter and rock star Lenine teamed up with pandeiro master and percussionist Marcos Suzano and recorded "Olho de Peixe" which re-revolutionized and popularized the pandeiro for a new generation. Suzano plays the pandeiro "reverse" starting on the tips and creates amazing grooves for each of the tracks on that album. He grew up listening to rock and interpreting drum set grooves for rock and funk onto the pandeiro. Below are a few basic funk grooves adapted for pandeiro.

Basic Funk pattern

t h t Th SL h t Th t Th t h SL h t h

Example 1: Funk Variation #1

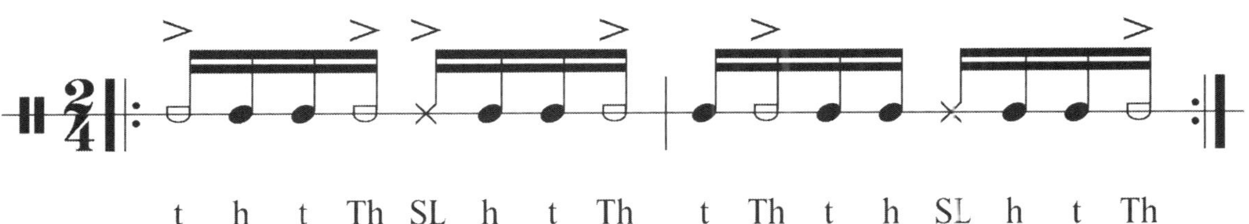

Example 2: Funk Variation #2

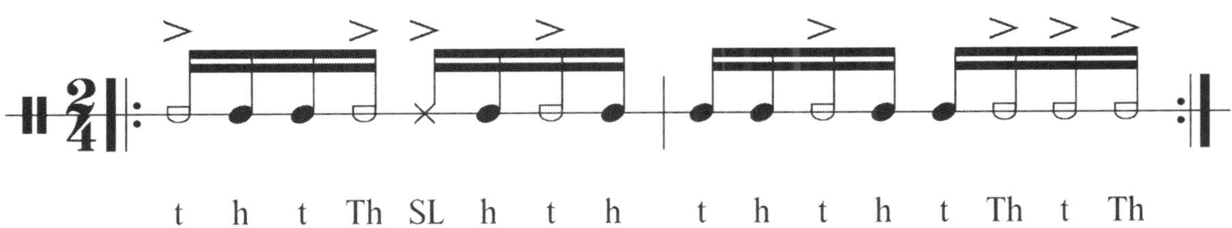

Example 3: Funk Variation #3

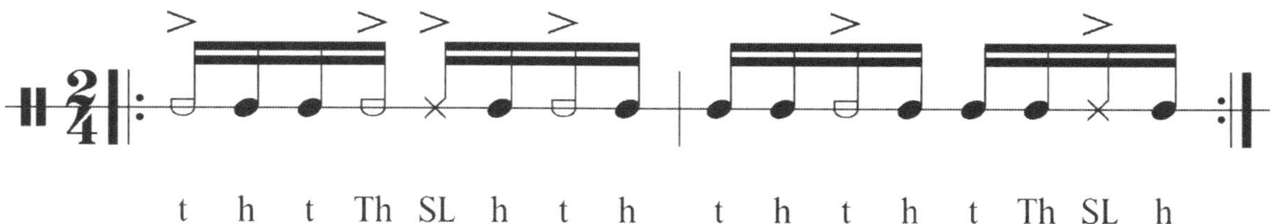

Example 4: Funk Variation #4

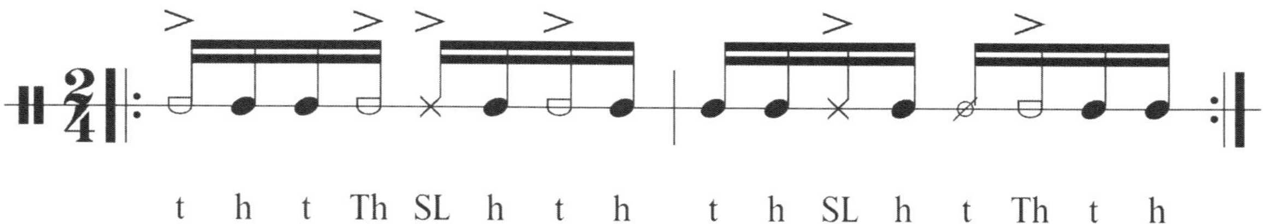

Funk Listening Suggestions

- *Olho de Peixe album by Lenine & Marcos Suzano*
- *Sambatown album by Marcus Suzano*
- *Pandeirando by Emerson Taquari*

Chapter 38. Americana Na E.P.M.: A Pandeiro Duet in Choro Form

AMERICANA

NA

E.P.M.

A Pandeiro Duet in Choro Form

By Ami Molinelli

AMERICANA NA E.P.M.

by Ami Molinelli

1. The order of the piece is ABBACA.

    a. The pandeiro is played with a choro in mind meaning 16th notes are in constant rotation with the left hand and the open tones are given utmost importance.

    b. The first time through the A section both players play the top staff in unison.

    c. The second time through the A section, play the two parts.

    d. The first time through the B section both players play the top staff in unison.

    e. The second time through the B section, play the two parts.

    f. The third time through the A section both players play the top staff in unison.

    g. In the C section each stave is played twice, with 2 bars of shaking played before the first time through. The players also switch parts on the second playing of each stave.

    h. The C section ends with alternating improvised solos. Measure 50 begins an 8-bar solo where one player is improvising while the other shakes the pandeiro horizontally in a constant 16th note rhythm. This 8-bar section repeats with the other player soloing the second time through. If players choose to repeat the sequence more than once it is up to their discretion. The next 4-bar solo section is played 4 times with the players switching parts each time through, one soloing while the other shakes, etc. This structure applies to the 2-bar solo, and the final 1-bar solo which is played a total of 4 times with players alternating parts each time.

    i. The C section is followed by one final playing of the A section at a faster tempo. The final A section begins on cue from the first soloist.

AMERICANA NA E.P.M.
by Ami Molinelli

Notation key

Closed hit

Open hit

Jingle Sweep

(*Sweep the hand along the outer rim of the pandeiro jingles*)

Slap

Pandeiro Roll

(*Roll the pandeiro in a constant 16th note pattern*)

AMERICANA NA E.P.M. by Ami Molinelli

Notation Key

This notation key is intended to assist players in understanding what the unique notation in this composition represents.

Figure 1

Represented in Figure 1:

1. The closed notehead on beat 1 labeled "TH" is a closed hit using the thumb.
2. The closed notehead labeled "t" is a "tip" hit
3. The closed notehead labeled "h" is a "heel" hit.
4. The open notehead labeled "TH" is an open hit using the thumb.
5. The notehead with an "X" is always a slap either with the tips or thumb.
6. The open triangle notehead is sweeping the hand along the outer rim of the pandeiro jingles.

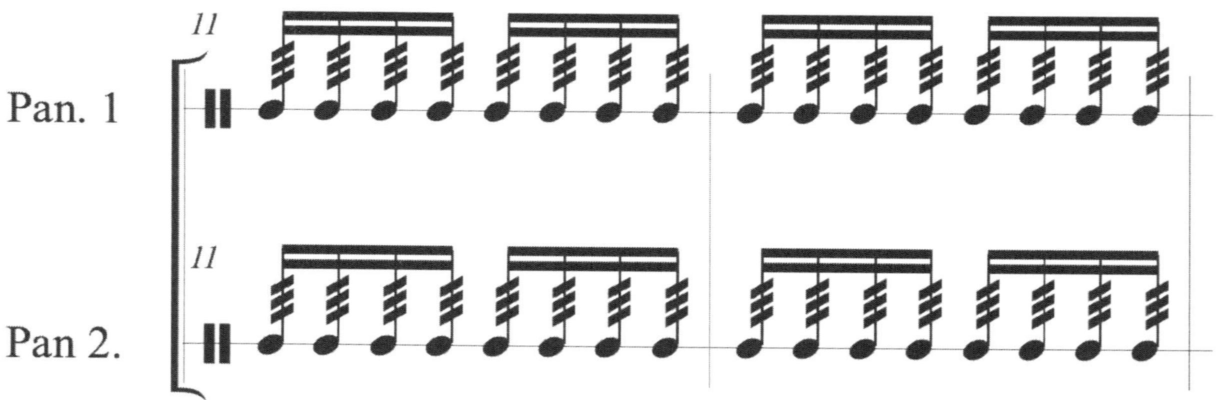

Figure 2

The notation in Figure 2 represents rolling the pandeiro in a constant 16th-note pattern. This notation appears at the end of the Introduction.

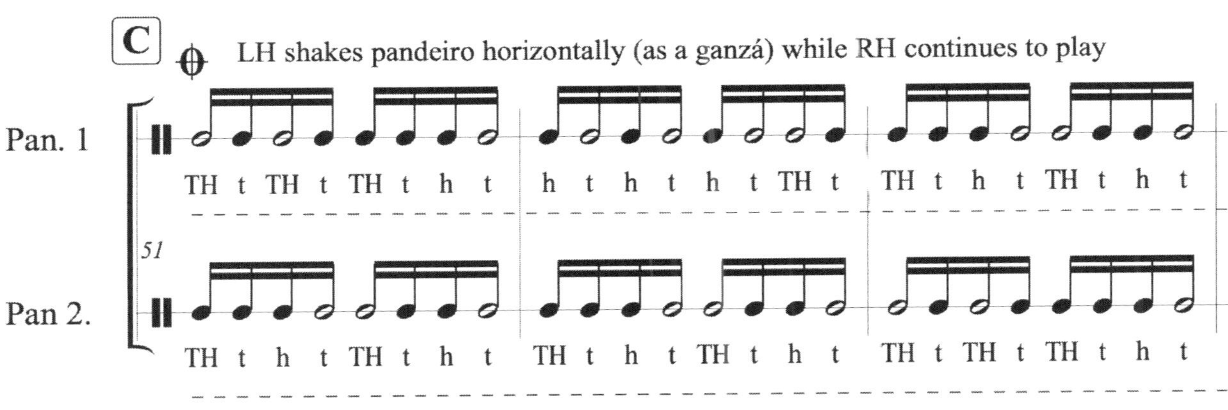

Figure 3

The notation in Figure 3 appears in the C Section. Throughout this entire section, both players shake the pandeiro horizontally (as a Brazilian shaker known as a ganzá with a supporting hand, as the dominant hand continues to play the rhythms with their fingertips. The 16th note figures were not notated throughout the entire section to make it easier for players to read the rhythms being played by the fingertips.

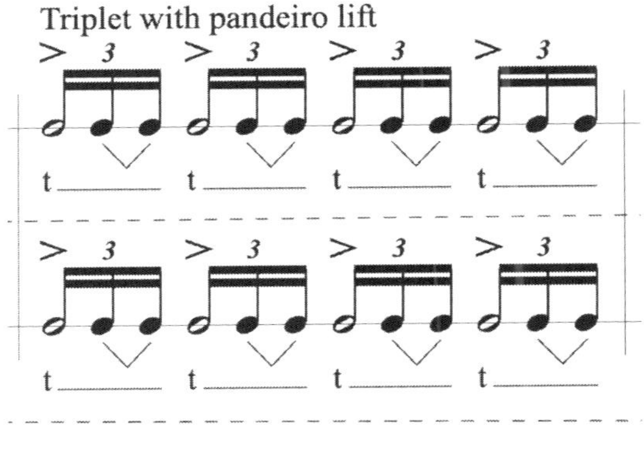

Figure 4

Figure 4 is seen in measure # 40 of the C section. It represents a triplet that is made by hitting the pandeiro tone and then lifting the arm holding the pandeiro upwards to make the successive triplet note sound with the jingle lifting up and then coming down from the rapid arm movement.

Americana Na E.P.M.

Ami Molinelli

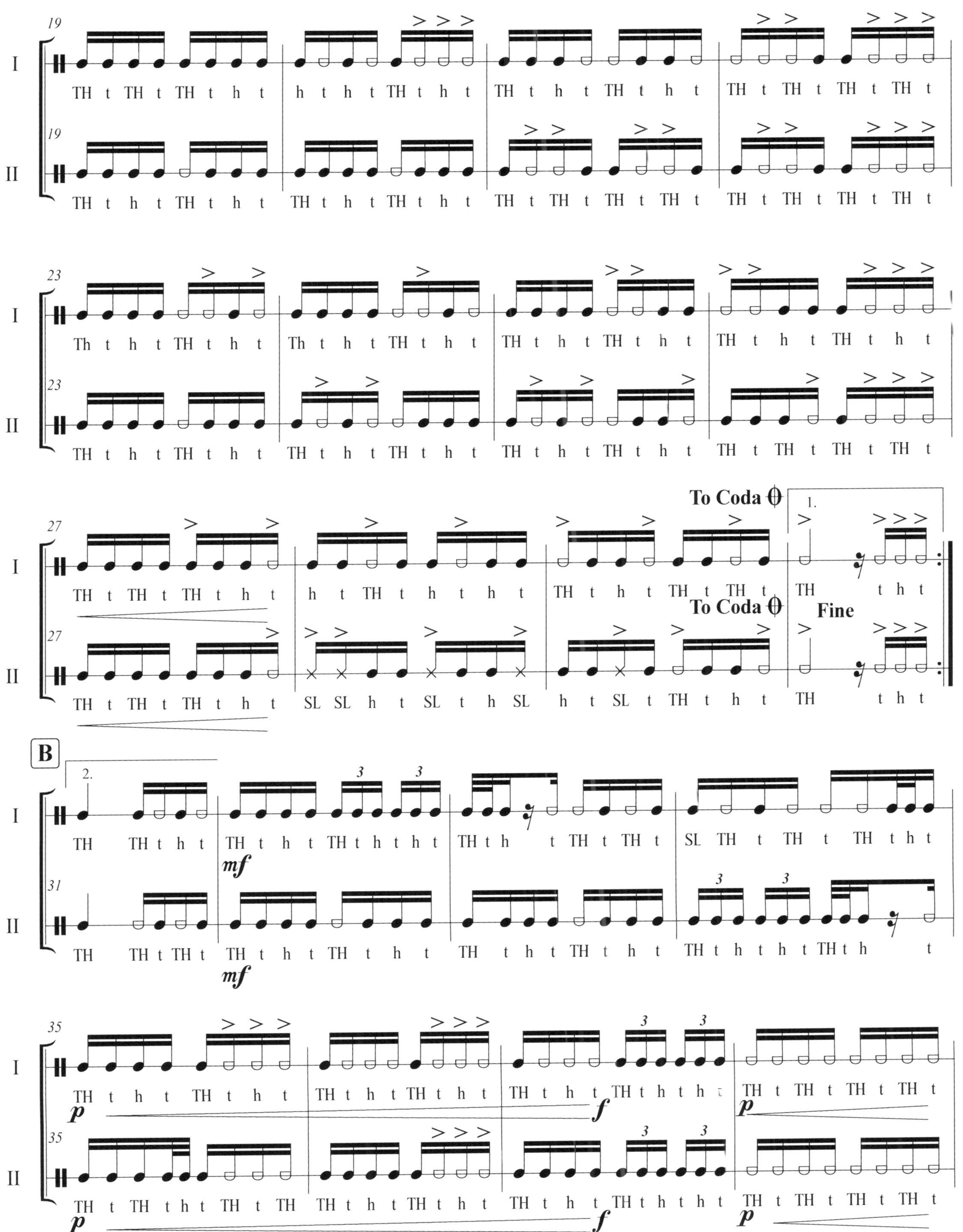
19
I
TH t TH t TH t h t h t h t TH t h t TH t h t TH t h t TH t TH t TH t TH t
II
TH t h t TH t h t TH t h t TH t h t TH t TH t TH t TH t TH t TH t TH t TH t
23
I
Th t h t TH t h t Th t h t TH t h t TH t h t TH t h t TH t h t TH t h t
II
TH t h t TH t h t TH t h t TH t h t TH t h t TH t h t TH t TH t TH t TH t
27
To Coda
1.
I
TH t TH t TH t h t h t TH t h t h t TH t h t TH t TH t TH t h t
To Coda
Fine
II
TH t TH t TH t h t SL SL h t SL t h SL h t SL t TH t h t TH t h t
B
2.
I
TH TH t h t TH t h t TH t h t h t TH t h t TH t TH t SL TH t TH t TH t h t
mf
31
II
TH TH t TH t TH t h t TH t h t TH t h t TH t h t TH t h t h t TH t h t
mf
35
I
TH t h t TH t h t TH t h t TH t h t TH t h t TH t h t h t TH t TH t TH t TH t
p f p
II
TH t TH t h t TH t TH TH t h t TH t h t TH t h t TH t h t h t TH t TH t TH t TH t
p f p

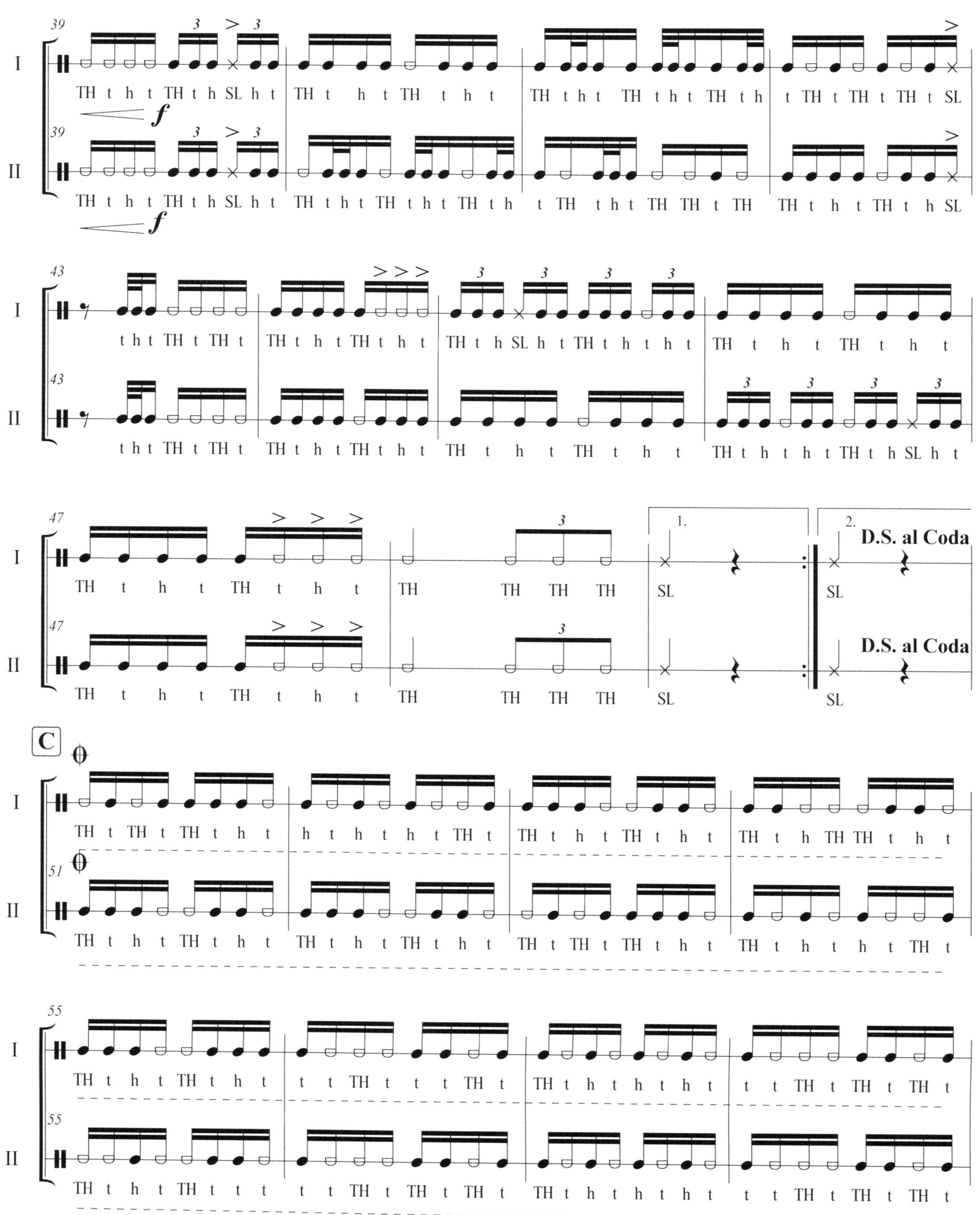
39
I
TH t h t TH t h SL h t | TH t h t TH t h t | TH t h t TH t h t TH t h | t TH t TH t TH t SL
f
II
TH t h t TH t h SL h t | TH t h t TH t h t TH t h | t TH t h t TH TH t TH | TH t h t TH t h SL
f
43
I
t h t TH t TH t | TH t h t TH t h t | TH t h SL h t TH t h t h t | TH t h t TH t h t
II
t h t TH t TH t | TH t h t TH t h t | TH t h t TH t h t | TH t h t h t TH t h SL h t
47
I
TH t h t TH t h t | TH TH TH TH | 1. SL | 2. SL
D.S. al Coda
II
TH t h t TH t h t | TH TH TH TH | SL | SL
D.S. al Coda
C
51
I
TH t TH t TH t h t | h t h t h t TH t | TH t h t TH t h t | TH t h TH TH t h t
II
TH t h t TH t h t | TH t h t TH t h t | TH t TH t TH t h t | TH t h t h t TH t
55
I
TH t h t TH t h t | t t TH t t t TH t | TH t h t h t h t | t t TH t TH t TH t
II
TH t h t TH t t t | t t TH t TH t TH t | TH t h t h t h t | t t TH t TH t TH t

I 77 One bar solo — One bar solo — D.C. al Fine

II 77 One bar solo — One bar solo — D.C. al Fine

Chapter 39. Pandeiro Maintenance and Frequently Asked Questions

How to Tune a Pandeiro

The tuning lugs hold the pandeiro in place and your pandeiro drum key is used to loosen or tighten the tension on the head of the pandeiro. Turning the drum key to the right tightens the tension and sound of the pandeiro and turning them to the left loosens it. The hotter it is outdoors the more chance your pandeiro will tighten with the climate and use. Be conscious of it and don't leave it in a car or by a windowsill where it would get direct sunlight.

Getting the Right Sound

I tend to like a more "bass" sounding pandeiro so once you start to get the technique of a bass tone you will find a tone that is appealing to you. If I'm playing with a band and there is a drummer and bass player, I tend to tune my pandeiro higher because my bass notes aren't as essential and it's more the ride/swing of the jingles that are important. If I'm playing choro and I'm the only percussionist, then my bass note is very important as it's playing the "surdo" or bass drum for the samba/choro feel.

Jingles

Pandeiro jingles are made with either chrome or brass. The biggest difference between an American tambourine and a Brazilian tambourine is that a Brazilian tambourine has concave jingles and an American tambourine has convex jingles. Some early American tambourines used in gospel and vaudeville used concave jingles but now most use convex. Brazilian choro pandeiros traditionally use brass or lighter aluminum jingles It has to do with volume and brightness. There are many ways to adjust or mute the sound of the jingles. Sometimes they are hammered to change the sound and dampen the brightness. In addition, there is a third jingle or metal spacer in between the jingles. Sometimes players put pieces of bottle caps sanded and flattened in the middle or different kinds of metal. Using a plastic mute that is sometimes slipped over the jingle on one side.

Taping the Bottom of the Pandeiro

People put tape on the bottom because it slightly cuts the overhead ringtones of the skin, and especially the jingles. Medical tape, packing tape or gaffer tape is good. Something that you can easily take off and won't strip off the skin of your pandeiro like duct tape. Don't use clear packing tape or duct tape but something with "paper" in it. There are several kinds of patterns to make including an X, square, * (asterisk) or other ideas. Place one piece of tape on the underside of the pandeiro at a time and test the sound until you have enough tape to hear a balanced sound you like. It's important to try the sound sequentially as you tape it up.

Protecting Your Hand

The drum is very small if your thumb or any part of your hand is hitting the rim or metal ring and hurting or bruising you are most definitely doing something wrong.

Wax to Get a Roll

Getting a roll can be achieved by licking the tip of your finger with saliva to get moisture. Using wax is another method. Be careful because you don't want to cover your drum too much so that it changes the sound. I prefer beeswax because it is natural and not synthetic and if you apply too much it scrapes off easily without changing the head of the drum. Some players use surfboard wax.

Your middle finger or thumb can make a roll. Make sure the pandeiro is perpendicular to your hand and that your fingers are stiff and not loose. Use the friction of the drum.

Microphones

There are continually going to be new ways to amplify your pandeiro as technology and audio gear improves. I like the clip-on microphone and use an audio tecnica clip-on microphone. The microphone clips on the bottom. Another way is to mic it from the bottom if you are using a microphone on a stand. (See Chapter 5 for more information on amplification.)

I prefer a clip-on microphone because when I use 16th note rotation it's difficult to play above a microphone consistently. Be advised to practice with the microphone on. It will add weight to your drum and if your left hand isn't used to it, you will get tired!

This will also benefit you in live performance, since you will know how your pandeiro should sound amplified.

Recording Your Pandeiro
There are several tutorials online but normally two microphones are used when recording. One underneath to get the bass notes and body of the drum and then an overhead microphone. Make sure that the microphone is centered underneath the drum. This can be a setup that is used live too if you don't have a clip-on microphone.

Cases

Protecting Your Pandeiro
Investing in a case for your pandeiro is a good idea as they are fragile instruments. Especially if your pandiero has a natural (non-synthetic) head, it will be sensitive to climate changes. Keeping it in a case is the best thing you can do to protect it. Never leave it somewhere where it will get very hot, like a car or by a window on a hot day, as it can heat up your drumhead and split the head easily.

Hard vs. Soft Cases
There are two kinds of cases for a pandeiro. Soft cases are more common. Hard cases made for a pandeiro are mostly made by Brazilian drum manufactures.

Tuning

How to Tune
Tuning a pandeiro is like tuning a snare or tom drum. Make sure that each lug is loosened evenly so that the frame of the drum doesn't become lopsided. ALWAYS loosen the pandeiro before you put it away.

1. Never leave a pandeiro in the sun or your car. If the skin gets too hot and tightens it will split.
2. Never tune only a few lugs, make it even.

When you tune the drum, you can do a quarter-inch turn on each if it's really "dead" sounding. Do a small turn on all of them either skipping each lug and then going back and tuning the skipped ones. (i.e., 1, 3, 5, 2, 4, 6) OR just doing a small turn all around. Then test it out and see if you like the sound. You will start to find the sound you like.

Where to purchase a pandeiro?
Pandeiros have come a long way manufactured outside of Brazil. Several companies internationally make choro pandeiros. Most choro pandeiros in Brazil are traditionally made by a luthier who is known for making them by hand. There are several different luthiers in Brazil such as Pizzott, Dyorman, and Rafael Toledo. In addition, there are Brazilian manufacturers like Gope or Contemporânea. Stateside there are several pandeiros being made by all the main percussion manufacturers such as Latin Percussion, Pearl, Remo, Meinl and Cooperman. The only American-made pandeiro by a luthier is the Bola Pandeiro. Bola is a luthier from the Bay Area and makes several Brazilian instruments by hand. There are also luthiers in Germany, Japan and worldwide!

Obrigada!

Thank you to my father, James P. Molinelli Sr., Jovino Santos Neto, Ted Falcon, and Michael Spiro for a preview and edits to this book. Thank you to Randy Gloss and Guello for their countless patience and instruction back at CalArts and for encouraging me to always take meticulous notes and use bound notebooks that will last as the years pass on. Randy Gloss challenged me to think of this pandeiro as an instrument that could play anything including non-western music notation and concepts for the pandeiro and anything I can get my hands on! Thank you to Marcos Suzano, Oscar Bolão, Celso Silva, Carlinhos Pandeiro de Ouro, and Durval Pereira for unlocking many facets of the pandeiro, history, musicality, and technique for me. Thank you to both Rogério Souza and Edinho Gerber for countless conversations on the intricacies of choro and for trusting me to accompany you on pandeiro. Thank you to the "Maestro," Rogério Souza for being a true mentor, not just of your encyclopedic knowledge of the choro but also of soul, swing and musicality. There is no replacement for a family legacy and history playing this music and the Souza family continues to pass on this legacy both in Rio de Janeiro, Brazil and abroad and it is a great honor to know you. Thank you to Tristan Aronovich who I met at the California Institute of the Arts, then a young classical Brazilian guitar performer from São Paolo, who introduced me to choro through our student trio and brought me weekly albums to digest and then discuss in all things Brazilian music. He also introduced me to Roberta Cunha Valente! Thank you to Roberta Cunha Valente who was as gracious to me when I first met her as she is now. Thank you to Dennis Broughton, Rich Rice, Jorge Alabê, and many others at California Brazil Camp who have fostered this cultural hot spot in the redwoods and fostered many a choro roda with the greats! Thank you to Bola who is the only luthier I know of in the U.S. making pandeiros and other wonderful Brazilian percussion instruments and helping supply pandeiros to new and emerging players! Thank you to Grupo Falso Baiano – Brian Moran, Zack Pitt-Smith, and Jesse Appelman with whom I have had the pleasure of learning and playing choro with since 2004. Thank you to the Berkeley Choro Festival for creating culture and a wonderful event that thrives! Thank you to Ted Falcon, Eduardo Souza and Katia Morães. Thank you to all the students and participants of Jazz Camp West and CBC who took my classes, asked questions, and spent weeks with me learning pandeiro so that this book was created with you all in mind and inspired and shaped by you. Thank you to Anne Sajdera for helping me with continual edits and work sessions and to help conceptualize this book and being an expert and aid in Finale. Thank you to Tajma Beverly who helped me with the very first draft of this book! Thank you to Joe Chellman for help with formatting and Andy Moqq for your support and aid and beautiful photography. Thank you to LP – Latin Percussion for their continued support and investment. Lastly, thank you to Mel Bay editors who made this instructional book even better.

Bibliography

Bolão, Oscar. “Batuque É Um Privelegio,” Rio de Janeiro, Lumiar Editora, 3rd Edition, Rio de Janeiro, BR; 2003

Bolão, Oscar, III Festival Nacional de Choro “Apostila de Percussão e Bateria.” Rio De Janeiro, 2007

Castro, Ruy, “The Story of the Brazilian Music That Seduced the World” Chicago Review Press 2003

III Festival Nacional de Choro, “Apostila de Historia Do Choro” Rio de Janeiro, BR: 2007

Sampãio, Luiz Roberto and Camargo, Victor. “Pandeiro Brasileiro.” Rio de Janeiro, BR; 2004

Caracas, Thomas George and Livingston, Tamara Elena, “Choro: A Social History of a Brazilian Popular Music” Bloomington, IN, US; 2005

Falcon, Ted, “Frevo: 20 Marchas e Frevos de Carnaval” Los Angeles, 2016

Fryer, Peter, “Rhythms of Resistance: African Musical Heritage in Brazil.” London: University Press of New England; 2000

Gloss, Randy, “Through the Looking Glass” Los Angeles, CA; 2007

Hoffman, Eric Interview Director of Maracatu Pacifico, September 5, 2022

Oliveira, Tito, “Afro-Brasileiros na Bateria” Salvador, Bahia, BR 2014

Pereira, Durval, “Ritmos Nordestinos” (Rio de Janeiro, RJ 2003-2007

Silva, Celsinho “Choro 100: Play Along Choro” Biscoito Fino, Rio de Janeiro, BR; 2008

Wright, Sarah, “The music of Lundu” Blog post for Latin Sensations website: https://latinsensations.wordpress.com/the-music-of-lundu-by-sarah-wright/

Interviews and lessons with: Guello, Rogério Souza, Edinho Gerber, Eduardo Souza, Ted Falcon, Jorge Alabê, Jovino Santos Neto, Carlinhos Pandeiro de Ouro, Durval Pereira, Marcos Suzano, Jovino Santos Neto. 2004-2024

About the Author

Ami Molinelli is a professional American percussionist and educator specializing in American (roots/pop/jazz), Brazilian and Latin music.

Ami received her Master of Fine Arts from the California Institute of the Arts. Her performance and recording credits include theater and television (NBC). She is endorsed by Latin Percussion (LP) and Rhythm Tech.

Her current musical project, “Raizes in Choro & Samba” with acclaimed guitar masters Rogério Souza and Edinho Gerber from Duo Violão Brasil + 1 features women composers and the intersection between choro and samba following their 2019 “História do Choro” album. (“Celebrated as one of the best jazz albums from the Bay Area.” Andy Gilbert, San Jose Mercury News) She is a three-time San Francisco Arts Commission Individual Artist Recipient and with DV+1 has been featured at the Chamber Music Association live showcase and are recipients of the South Arts Jazz Roads grant.

She co-leads the Brazilian and Jazz ensemble, Grupo Falso Baiano with three albums to their credit: “Depois” released in 2017, “Simplicidade – Live at Yoshi’s”, and “Viajando em Choro e Jazz.” Grupo Falso Baiano has been featured on NPR’s the California Report, Radio Latina and Pandora LIVE!

Her percussion curriculum has been used and published in clinics and educational workshops including the Los Angeles Philharmonic, The San Francisco Jazz Center, Los Angeles Music Center, Young Audiences of Northern California, UFBA Ouro Preto, Brasil, HeadStart (San Mateo County), Los Angeles Music Academy, California Brazil Camp, Jazz Camp West, etc. She is cofounder and director of **Music Is First!** a music and literacy integration non-profit reaching under-served early education classrooms in the Bay Area so that the youngest learners have access to music.

Ami has performed and recorded with artists such as Jovino Santos Neto, Guello, Michael Spiro, John Santos, Rogério Souza and Duo Violão, Jai Uttal, George Duke, Teka, José Neto, Kenny Washington, Billy Hart, Nilson Mattá, Josh Nelson, and more.

Ami proudly is endorsed by Latin Percussion and Rhythm Tech.

Other Mel Bay Percussion Books

Bodhran

Bodhran: The Basics (Woods)
Bodhran: Beyond the Basics (Woods)
Bodhran Grooves (Woods)

Bongo

Bongo Drumming: Beyond the Basics (Salloum)
Conga and Bongo Drum in Jazz (Salloum)
First Lessons Bongo (Salloum)
Fun with Bongos (Salloum)
School of Bongo (Salloum)
The Art of Bongo Drumming DVD with Special Feature by Armando Peraza (Salloum)
The Bongo Book (Salloum)

Cajon

First Lessons Cajon (Perlson)
Studies for Cajon (Rottger)
The Rhythm Encyclopedia (Woods)

Conga

Afro-Cuban Percussion Play-Along (Salloum)
Afro-Cuban Rhythms: Gig Savers Complete Edition (Salloum)
Bembe Conversations (Rodriguez)
Conga and Bongo Drum in Jazz (Salloum)
First Lessons Conga (Salloum)
Rumba Soloing Technique Vol. 1. (Brooks)
Rumba: Afro-Cuban Conga Drum Improvisation Vol. 2 (Brooks)
Tomás Cruz Conga Method Vol. 1: Cuban Conga Technique
Tomás Cruz Conga Method Vol. 2: Essential Conga Rhythms
Tomás Cruz Conga Method Vol. 3: Timba - Modern Conga Rhythms
Traditional Afro-Cuban Concepts in Congtemporary Music (Rodriguez)
The Rhythm Encyclopedia (Woods)

Darbuka

Magnificent Darbuka Rhythms Chart

Djembe

First Lessons Djembe (Mattioli)
The Rhythm Encyclopedia (Woods)

Tabla

Learning the Tabla (Courtney)
Learning the Tabla Vol. 2. (Courtney)

Frame Drum/Tambourine/Riqq

Classical Riqq Technique (Baklouk/LeCorgne)
Pandiero Method (Molenia)
Playing the Frame Drum (Woods)
Rhythm is the Cure (Belloni)

WWW.MELBAY.COM

WWW.MELBAY.COM